A Struggle for the Irish American Dream

Based on My Parent's Lives

Diane Lyne Gasparrini

A STRUGGLE FOR THE IRISH AMERICAN DREAM
BASED ON MY PARENT'S LIVES

iUniverse books may be ordered through booksellers or by contacting:

iUniverse
1663 Liberty Drive
Bloomington, IN 47403
www.iuniverse.com
844-349-9409

Because of the dynamic nature of the internet, any web addresses or links contained in this book may have changed since publication and may no longer be valid. The views expressed in this work are solely those of the author and do not necessarily reflect the views of the publisher, and the publisher hereby disclaims any responsibility for them.

Any people depicted in stock imagery provided by Getty Images are models, and such images are being used for illustrative purposes only. Certain stock imagery © Getty Images.

ISBN: 978-1-6632-3343-1 (sc)
ISBN: 978-1-6632-3344-8 (e)

Library of Congress Control Number: 2022918099

Print information available on the last page.

iUniverse rev. date: 11/18/2022

Contents

Acknowledgment

I would like to thank my fourth cousin, Gerard Lyne, a noted Irish historian, for all the research he has done on our ancestors.

Preface

Though the people of Ireland love their native land, during the nineteenth and twentieth centuries, many felt compelled to leave it for a variety of reasons. Despite this decision, they longed for their birthplace forever. It may not have the warmth and beauty of French beaches or the history of Rome, but it does have its own personal charisma, which lures its emigrants and their descendants, back and now quite successfully keeps the natives at home. Despite its majestic mountains and cliffs that tower over the sea, the exceptional scenery is not what draws emigrants back. It is the warmth of its people and their fierce loyalty and love of home that brings them back, even generations later, to the small island that lies just west of England.

Very early in Ireland's history, the Celts arrived. These great warriors, who had spread across Europe, eventually landed on the distant shore of an island to the northwest of Europe. They brought with them their language and storytelling traditions, which were readily adopted by the natives. As a polytheistic community, the Celts enjoyed their own feasts and celebrated the changing of the seasons, beginning with the summer solstice, the longest day of the year. On this feast day, they honored their goddesses, drank, and ate, hoping for a bountiful harvest. Some of these customs were adopted by the natives, but they lost their popularity with the introduction of Christianity. Days honoring saints replaced them, such as Saint Brigid's Day, which occurs on the first day of spring. The Irish have also retained their beautiful designs, which they craft in stone, metal, and many other materials, as seen in the Celtic cross.

Christianity was introduced to Ireland before AD 400, with the arrival of the monks who built monasteries all over the country and converted the Celtic people. Saint Patrick, who actually arrived from Britain as a slave, was part of that change to Christianity. He became a bishop in the church and a major influence on the Celts. He is credited with using the shamrock to explain the trinity. One shamrock with three leaves symbolizes three people in one God. This image has taken on other meanings since then, but that was his Christian interpretation.

Monasteries spread all over Ireland. This included the one on Skellig Michael, a small craggy island off the coast of Kerry, where the monks were intentionally isolated. The men lead very difficult, demanding lives. Their major goal was to pray in the Christian faith that they followed and to escape the distractions of the world. Among their other duties, they encouraged scholarship and fashioned ornately detailed books to preserve the gospels, Celtic poetry, and history. They took on the responsibility of copying and preserving famous works like the *Book of Kells*, which contains all four gospels and is now in Trinity College. They also worked with precious metals to design chalices and other religious necessities, which were used in their monastic lives. Scholars were encouraged to join them, and they could often be found studying with the monks.

This period in Ireland is sometimes viewed as the Golden Age. The monks preserved the scholarship of Europe. Many joined them in their pursuit of God and knowledge. Some believe that during this era you couldn't "swing a cat in Ireland without hitting a saint" (Blackwell, 2004). Many of these monasteries still exist such as Glendalough and Clonmacnoise, which are now in ruins. Saints were plentiful in Ireland; thus it became the land of saints and scholars and a haven of peace and learning while Europe was dealing with the barbarians. But by AD 700–800, the Vikings returned to Ireland seeking the treasures of the monasteries, which had been created by the monks. At times more aggressive than others, the Vikings settled in several cities, including Dublin and Waterford. According to recent DNA discoveries, there is considerably more variety in the Irish gene pool than we realized, particularly Scandinavian genes (McKeown, 2018).

The Norman invasion of the twelfth century also had a lasting effect on Ireland. The Normans, who came from northern France, mingled with the ruling class in Britain, creating a powerful enemy whose goal was to conquer Ireland. William the Conqueror, a descendant of the

Normans, conquered and eventually became the king of England. His descendant King Henry II invaded Ireland in AD 1171 because he feared that the English lords who had property in Ireland seemed too comfortable with the Irish way of life. He won, but these same lords were welcomed back once they promised loyalty to the king. Many of them built castles to protect themselves from the natives. Ultimately, Henry was in control of parts of Ireland for years to come. This signaled the beginning of English dominance for centuries. Many Norman lords also retained power, but unlike King Henry, some of the Norman lords became part of the Irish culture.

Invasions from other countries continued on several fronts, including the Scots, the French, Britain's King Henry VIII, and Oliver Cromwell who reduced the population of Ireland enormously. This small island defended itself from numerous armies and ships while life continued for its remaining citizens, as they worked the land, raised their cattle, and tried to survive.

In the seventeenth century, England took an even bolder stand in Ireland and attempted to totally control it because England feared that its enemies might try to reach the empire through Ireland. Englishmen in Ireland had already been forbidden to speak Irish or intermarry with the natives. Now a new level of animosity was aimed at Irish subjects. Some nations bore England's demands with a more submissive attitude, but Ireland refused.

When the Reformation occurred, King Henry VIII broke off from the Catholic church and the pope. He also declared himself head of the Church of England. This brought on a new wave of legal bigotry and the adoption of penal laws. Some of this animosity had been in place for years, but now it was spelled out in detail. These individual laws prevented practicing Roman Catholics from holding offices or owning land. They could not travel more than five miles from their homes or bear arms, and they prevented Catholics from teaching or running schools. These aggressive measures only made the natives more determined to cling to their Catholicism and to fight their long-hated enemy while England sought total control of Ireland.

Against this background, Dr. Dermot Lyne, whose family fled to Catholic Spain with O'Sullivan-Beare, returned to the Beare peninsula in southwest Kerry and Cork. Many other chieftains also fled to other Catholic countries. During their absence, Sir William Petty had gained a great deal of land in Cork and Kerry due to his loyalty to Cromwell. Ironically, his son was now selling leases to these lands to descendants of former owners. Despite the bad blood that existed between the Irish and English, Richard Orpen, an agent for Sir William Petty's son, leased these properties mostly to Irish Catholics. Thus, in the latter part of the century, Dr. Lyne, along with twenty other Irish Catholics, leased lands in Ireland. Lyne settled in County Kerry (Lyne 2006).

Within this oppressive atmosphere, the Lyne family fought many battles to hold onto their farms. Each generation dealt with the new restrictions that the crown created, often through the court system. There were instances where their silence in court permitted them to keep their farms. But after several generations, the original property purchased by Dr. Lyne had been divided so many times among his descendants that his heirs inherited much smaller farms that were now scattered on the Beara Peninsula.

The Lyne family of Eskadour was one branch of this family, which proudly continued the farming tradition. In the latter half of the nineteenth century, their eldest boy, Joseph, was due to inherit the farm. The next in line, Richard, was away at school when a catastrophe occurred: Joseph died. Now Richard would inherit his brother's prize. This arrangement hurt both young men; Joseph obviously lost his life, but Richard lost the life that he had envisioned for himself. He loved school and studying, some thought for the priesthood. As the next in line, he had to leave school and return to his rightful place as the owner of the farm in Eskadour. In the nineteenth century, inheriting a farm wasn't a casual gift but a serious responsibility. The Lyne family had fought hard to keep their land, and Richard wouldn't forfeit it. That change took place when Richard was almost twenty. For the next twenty-four years, he lived alone, worked on the farm, and studied whenever possible. Though he loved Ireland and all its traditions, this difficult and demanding occupation was his constant concern. Being up at dawn and working until dusk occupied many of his youthful years, until a sudden event changed his life.

At a social function in Kenmare, Richard was introduced to Helena O'Sullivan from County Cork. She was at least twenty years younger and full of life. Her positive, bright spirit gave him a new interest in life and a sense of wonder. She was warm, lovable, and admired by many. Luckily, Richard was perceptive enough to recognize her value. With this introduction, life was no longer lonely, and the future appeared promising. He was clever enough to charm the lovely Helena, and they wed in February 1901. They worked the farm together, and she bore healthy children, who were almost as outgoing as their mother. Yes, Richard's life had changed for the better but not forever.

Chapter 1

Survival

Helena O'Sullivan and Richard Lyne enjoyed many years together in their small stone home with their twelve children, who enriched their lives enormously. Margaret, the oldest, would later reign as the matriarch of the family well into her nineties. Her birth was followed by the births of Mary, Daniel, Richard, Helena, John, Sheila, Jeremiah, the twins Philip and Michael, Nora, and Christopher. Despite their humble home, this large Catholic family worked, prayed, and laughed together. They believed that their idyllic life would go on forever.

Before dawn on this particular morning, John, the sixth of Helena and Richard's children, rose early to track down a missing lamb, just as Da (Richard) had requested. The creature had been lost for days. The boys had kept a watchful eye out for it all that time, but they had been unable to find it. The family could not afford the loss of such a valuable animal, so John had been chosen to track it down, no matter how long it took. Though very young, he had shouldered more and more responsibility lately, so Da's request came as no surprise. His father had caught the flu three or four days earlier. It had destroyed every ounce of his energy and had confined him to bed. As head of the household, he still provided direction on managing the farm, but his children assumed all the chores, hoping he would overcome this debilitating illness.

John dressed quietly to avoid disturbing his parents and eleven brothers and sisters and walked softly to the front door. As he opened it, he glanced down at the Kenmare Bay, which flowed quietly alongside the farm, and admired the mighty Knockatee hills beyond the bay, veiled by a thick layer of fog. In the distance, the Atlantic Ocean, brooding and dark, shared its frequently harsh and unpredictable moods with the mountainous County Kerry. Though the air was cold, John ignored his discomfort and began his ascent up Stickeen Mountain, which was adjacent to his home. He was always on the alert for traces of the lamb or anything unusual that might explain its absence. He searched the crevices in the rocks where other lambs had become trapped in the past, turned to observe the source of any sound, and with every few steps, scanned the mountain as far as he could see in the distance. He continued his search for about an hour, without any luck.

Although he had been unsuccessful, he pursued his task. He was anxious to return with good news. His family needed that now. His eyes were focused, but his mind drifted as he considered the many generations before him who had traveled this farm and kept sheep. Despite the challenging climate and topography of this mountainous terrain, the Kerry people seemed able to endure any difficulty that came their way. In fact, not only had they grown accustomed to the difficulties that nature presented, but they were even strengthened in many ways by these hardships.

The farm, cows, and sheep needed a great deal of attention, but the children helped whenever possible. Their parents modeled the skills that were necessary to keep the farm running and the family fed. Eskadour was a farming community, and the children only knew this way of life. They pursued it with enthusiasm and the constant cheer of their mother. Life on the Lyne's farm was a safe and loving atmosphere for children and adults alike, until now.

As the sky brightened, searching for the missing lamb became easier, and John was able to relax as he continued his ascent. Though vigilant in his pursuit, John thought he heard someone cautioning him, "This is no time to take it easy, John. The poor creature must be half-starved." The words echoed his father's sentiments, but he recognized the voice of his little brother. John turned to see Jeremiah approaching. "Mam sent me to help you. I hope we're lucky enough to find him early so we can get back for breakfast. I'm starving."

Delighted to see a familiar face, John replied with a grin, "You're always starving. It's the lamb we're worried about." Jeremiah laughed, and the two brothers continued the search together, leaving twenty feet between them as they moved farther up the mountain, covering as much territory as possible.

"It's a bad morning to hunt the fella down," John remarked.

"We haven't had a fine day in almost a week," observed Jeremiah.

Trying to sound casual, John asked his brother, "Was Da out of bed when you left?"

"No, he was still sleeping. Mam kept us all quiet to avoid waking him. Lena carried the baby around so he wouldn't cry," admitted Jeremiah sadly.

Would Da ever be the same, John wondered. The mention of their father's condition changed John's mood. The joy of having some help in his quest faded as he thought of the grim reality that the family faced. His beloved home had changed enormously with Da's sickness.

Though frustrated by his weak body, Da had no choice but to remain in bed, perspiring, sleeping on and off, and eating very little. Their rare glimpses of him made them all anxious. Mam had sent for the doctor and nervously awaited his arrival, but the illness had spread. Yesterday Danny, the boys' oldest brother, exhibited similar symptoms. This life-threatening flu had spread throughout Kenmare, and it was now residing in their home, which was tucked against the *hilleen* (small hill). The sickness seemed unmerciful and unstoppable. With so many children in the family, some type of cold or fever had become a normal part of their lives, but the flu this year had killed people in the community. Children had disappeared from the one-room schoolhouse, and wakes had become a weekly occurrence. John was well aware of the changes. He feared losing his loved ones.

Jeremiah suddenly beckoned John over to him as he placed his finger over his lips. John listened for a moment and heard the complaints of the lamb. They followed the sound and discovered the missing member of the flock caught in a narrow gap in the rock. Lifting it gently, John examined it. Once he was sure the animal had not been harmed, he encouraged his brother to head home for breakfast. Surprised, Jeremiah asked, "But where are you going? Aren't you hungry?"

"I am hungry, but I think I'll bring the lamb down to the lower field to join the flock. Tell Mam I'll be home soon." Acquiescing to his brother's wishes, Jeremiah began his descent toward the house while John headed for the flock that was gathered by the bay.

Once he reached the field where the remaining sheep were grazing, he placed the lost lamb on the ground and watched the contented animal join the others. The wool from these animals had provided an income for the family for generations, so it was important for them to thrive. Most nearby farms raised sheep as well, so they shared the benefits of the mountains with their neighbors. The small houses that dotted the landscape harbored large families like his own. Periodic visits to these neighbors made him aware of their love of the land and commitment to it, just like his father's love and commitment. Although farming might be difficult, he was well aware of the blessings that his family enjoyed.

Lost in thought as he wandered along the bay, John noticed a stick and flung it as high as he could. Then he scrambled to catch it before it hit the ground. He could see the fog rolling over the mountain, approaching the field, and dampening his clothing. Walking alone soothed his anxiety, but he couldn't control his thoughts of Da. Though John had grown up believing that his father was invulnerable, he realized that Da was no longer young. He hadn't even become a father until his midforties. In the latter half of the nineteenth century, his Uncle Joseph had died, so his father had inherited the farm. Richard shared this history with his children often so that they would appreciate the farm and respect the land.

Raising twelve children while struggling to work the land was very demanding, and the strain was evident at times. His boys helped him whenever school wasn't in session, but Da insisted they pursue their studies. He had enjoyed learning and the camaraderie of the academic world. It had given him a great deal of satisfaction, and he mourned the loss of his academic pursuits. He wanted his children to have the same attitude toward their own educations.

Absorbed in his thoughts, John tossed the stick as high as he could and ran to retrieve it again. He moved across the fields and focused on the water as the wind rushed over the rocky terrain. Running killed the next half hour and provided some peace in his soul.

As he approached the Kenmare Castletownbere Road that ran along the bay, John was still tossing his stick in the air when he heard the neighing of a horse in the distance. Presuming he would spot a neighbor traveling along the road, he quickly turned with a ready greeting, but he was shocked when he recognized the carelessly mismatched black-and-tan uniforms of British soldiers.

The Royal Irish Constabulary, the police that were under the control of Britain, had lost a great deal of power after the Easter Rising of 1916. From that point on, the Irish favored their independence more than ever. They were moving toward a war for independence. To gain back their power, the British organized and sent a new force, the Black and Tans, who were men of questionable backgrounds. According to the British, they were in Ireland to control the IRA, but John often heard his parents discussing their aggressive measures, which became worse as the years went on. The paper gave many accounts of innocent farmers who were victimized by them. Rumor had it that they would carelessly shoot anyone in their paths.

Aware of the danger, John fell to the ground and crawled to a large rock, which was just ten feet away. Attempting to conceal himself, he crouched behind it hoping his quick response had eluded their watchful eyes. As he knelt there tensely, his entire being was consumed with the sounds of the horses. His body trembled as he listened to their approach. The clip-clop of the horses' hooves grew louder until they suddenly stopped. Then he heard nothing. Suddenly a soldier in a gruff English accent commanded, "Put it down, or we'll shoot!" John was astonished. *Were they talking to him? Was his stick so threatening?* He remained perfectly still, until he heard a gun cocked and the same voice repeat the threat, "Drop that gun, or I'll fire!" Now he understood that the newspapers were right. *These men had no scruples. Despite his youth, they threatened his life.*

Frightened but determined to appear fearless, he stepped into view and faced the invaders. Three of the five men had their guns aimed directly at him. Those behind them proudly bore condescending expressions. They were ready to pounce. Even though he was less than ten years old, John was confronting a new force that had been created by an old enemy. There was no one within shouting distance, so he remained silent. If he wished to live, he must stand his ground. The soldiers mumbled among themselves, obviously aware of their error. They glared at the boy in disappointment that they had only captured a child carrying a stick and not a man bearing a weapon.

"Where's your father?" shouted the leader. John couldn't speak. He looked down at the ground while desperately trying to compose himself. Then it suddenly struck him. *They are ashamed to attack me because of my age, so now they plan to go after Da.* He had spent the last hour fearing that an illness might snatch his father away and praying for his survival, so he certainly wouldn't assist these notorious murderers in hunting him down. The paralyzing fear seemed to subside once he considered the alternatives. In its place, there rose a wave of raging anger. These brutal beasts were unfit to even walk among his countrymen.

Slowly he raised his head, glared at the men, and in a mocking, shrill voice bellowed the words of a poem that he had learned in school, which condemned them, calling them awful names. "Beware of the thing that is coming, beware of the risen people, Who shall take what ye would not give.... Did ye think to conquer the people? Ye that have bullied and bribed, tyrants, hypocrites, liars!" (Pearse 1922). Out of nowhere, an infuriated soldier grabbed him by the collar, threw him down, and tossed his stick into the distance. The others encircled him, poking, kicking, and taunting the boy who had dared to voice his disdain. Stunned, John struggled to get up despite an injured leg, but he was unable to. Alone and hurt, he awaited their next move.

In an attempt to save face and gain some semblance of military order, the lead soldier, with a scowl that revealed his repulsion, repeated the question. "Where's your father, boy? These men have been pushed far enough."

"He must come from the house on the hill," remarked another. "We can search it and find his father ourselves. If he's not there, he's sure to be in the fields." The leader immediately agreed, and the group proceeded toward their horses, apparently to begin the search. They put away their guns, had a quick drink, and mounted their horses.

While listening to this change of plans, John grew more apprehensive since he was aware of Da's physical state. He looked up at the men who had just injured him and understood that they had no human compassion. *Their primitive view of the world was limited to kill or be killed. To them, we are worthless.* In a last-ditch effort, John yelled, "My Da has the black flu," which was a phrase the newspapers used to describe the flu of 1918. He admitted it to himself and them. Da's illness would probably kill him. Their facial expressions changed immediately. They all stopped and looked at each other but did not utter a sound. They too were aware of the many deaths caused by this ravaging illness. The soldiers glanced at their leader. He ignored them, slowly turned his horse around, and headed farther down the road. The others quietly followed him without making eye contact. They were no longer interested in John or his father. As they left, a few gazed loathingly at the boy whom they were leaving behind. He remained on the ground and watched as they went in search of another victim. He had been fortunate enough to survive this threat, but he wondered if Da would be as lucky.

After his encounter with the Black and Tan soldiers, John limped halfway home. Knocking him down had done more damage than he realized. His painful leg was bleeding enough to stain his pants. The left side of his face ached, but he was not sure why. Stunned by the aggressive behavior of the soldiers, he kept replaying the scene in his mind. Though he had read about the Black and Tans in the newspaper and heard stories, his personal encounter at their hands was a shock and a serious warning to a young man who had always felt so secure and safe in Eskadour and Kenmare. However, he would definitely keep this from his parents. Life at home was challenging enough for his family without taking on the Black and Tans.

Just as he reached the road to his house, he saw three of his brothers racing toward him and screaming, "John," over and over as loud as they could. Jeremiah and the twins, Michael and Philip, dashed to the bottom of the road yelling questions as they came.

Jeremiah demanded to know, "Where have you been all this time? Mam has been worried."

John was happy to see them, but he didn't have time to respond before Michael made a few demands too. "What happened to your leg? We watched you limping the whole way. Did someone do this to you?" John began to explain the version of the story that he was willing to share. Then he noticed Philip, who had only listened thus far, staring at his damaged leg.

Finally, Philip said, "I think you may be seriously hurt, John. Lean on my shoulder, and we'll go up to the house." The others followed his lead. Jeremiah grabbed John's other arm, and they assisted their older brother up to the house. He could relax now that he was home again.

As they approached the house, they saw their sister Sheila busily feeding the chickens. She glanced in their direction and ran to them asking, "What's happened? Are you all right? Where have you been?"

"I left early this morning and finally found that missing sheep." Turning to Jeremiah but still addressing Sheila, John asked, "Didn't Jeremiah tell you?"

Sheila laughed. "This is the first time I've seen him this morning. Richard and I are now in charge of the chickens. We've been busy all morning." Glancing down, she added, "That leg looks very bad, but Mam will know what to do." Richard, who came up from the barn at that moment, had been named after his father. He was older than the others and tall for his age. Although he was industrious, he was also a bit of a dreamer. Deep in his soul, he hoped that one day, he would go to America to find his fortune. He and Sheila returned to their tasks, and the others headed for the house.

When the four brothers finally opened the front door, Mam was delighted to see her missing son step over the threshold. That quickly disappeared when she noticed the blood on his leg where his pants had been torn. The brothers tried to explain how they had come upon John, but with one quick look, they were immediately quieted by their mother, who approached John asking, "Dear God, lad, how did this happen?"

"I fell," he uttered in a soft tone, ashamed that he wasn't revealing the entire truth to his mother. Mam escorted John over to the chair, grabbed a cloth from the press, and gently began cleaning the wound.

"Did you fall climbing the hill, John? This is such a deep cut," his mother commented sympathetically as she washed his leg.

"No, Mam. I tripped running through the field above the bay. I'm sorry I tore my pants." His sisters had gathered around him to witness the family's latest calamity.

Mary placed a hand on her brother's shoulder and reassured him. "Just a bit of a wound, John."

Lena, with baby Christopher in tow, remarked, "Sure, you'll be fine, John, once you master walking." They laughed, and once they were convinced that he was going to be fine, they returned to their individual responsibilities.

As his mother tended to the wound, the boys were absorbed in her skillful care. At first, John was preoccupied with his own wounds, but as he glanced around the room, he noticed his siblings absorbed in household duties. While Margaret pared the potatoes next to Mary, who was washing the vegetables, they didn't speak to each other, which was very unusual for these two. In the corner by the settee, Lena was changing the baby with little Nora by her side, but again, they did not say a word. Despite the number of people in the room who were engaged in a variety of chores, the house was almost quiet.

Now he was convinced that the flu had totally changed their lives. A new mood had transformed their happy household. It had been full of laughter and good cheer. Now it was a soundless mausoleum, full of repressed children, enduring a major catastrophe in their lives—the possible loss of their father and brother. They all knew that in the next room their sick loved ones were trying to sleep and overcome this ravishing illness.

He thought, *No wonder the younger boys yelled so loudly as they ran to meet me. Everyone is so careful not to mention the illness. They can't express any feelings.* The worry and silence made them all uncomfortable. They bore a serious burden for such young people. The stressful atmosphere overpowered the household.

When Mam had finished bandaging John's leg, she found another pair of pants for him and gave him breakfast. He quickly devoured every morsel. He had been starving after his long trek up the mountain.

Mam cleared the table and asked him to follow her to the barn. Though he was not quite sure why they were going there, he did as he was told.

They walked slowly in that direction and then Mam, with Herculean strength, faced John and said, "We've relied on you, your brothers, and your sisters for several days now, so I think you should know how your Da is faring. The doctor came from Kenmare this morning and confirmed your Da's diagnosis. He said the flu of last spring seemed a bit milder, but this new flu is stronger and devastating Kenmare. He gave us little hope." A tear slid down her cheek as she attempted to continue, but just then, Margaret suddenly appeared and took her mother's hand as Mam went on. "This morning, once the doctor left, I shared some of this with the others, but I want to make sure you know as well since you've been such a great help to Da."

John felt his mother's pain. Tears filled his eyes and flowed down his cheeks. *So now it has been confirmed. My father and brother are dying.* He hugged her, hoping to soothe her sorrow and his own.

Then attempting to control her voice, she added, "We've kept the children away from the back room where Da and Daniel are resting. We'll keep the younger ones busy outside or just in the kitchen. The rest of us will take turns visiting Da and Daniel quietly, with a meal and a prayer." So the plan was set in motion. In addition to going to school and manning the farm, each of them had to find a moment to say goodbye.

A darkened atmosphere pervaded the house for the next few days. The tiny house, often bursting with the noise and joy of twelve children, was always solemn now. Milking the cows and feeding the chickens remained the children's responsibilities before school. After school, the barn and chicken coop needed cleaning, the water had to be brought home, and they needed more peat for the fire. It was a never-ending litany of tasks. Mam prepared the meals for the family on an open hearth, which was no small accomplishment, and took care of Da and Daniel in her own gentle, loving way. She never revealed her sorrow to the young ones. Following Mam's suggestions, each of them found their moment to talk to their loved ones and try to lift their spirits. Though their appetites had almost disappeared, just the presence of family members seemed to improve their condition.

John held out the longest. It seemed unimaginable that he would ever say goodbye to his father and brother, but the priest had been in to give them last rites. John had a long conversation with his mother and finally brought in their dinners. Though barely audible, their warm greetings of, "Thank God for the man with the food," stole his heart. He sat for a chat while helping each of them swallow a few sips of soup and a bit of bread. He stayed with them until Daniel fell asleep. Only then, did his father raise his saddened eyes and speak in a hoarse, low voice. "This won't be easy for any of us, John, but I'm relying on you to support your mother. Whatever she says, agree and assist her. Do I have your word?"

"Don't worry, Da. I'll always take care of her." When Da smiled and closed his eyes, John left the room.

The next morning, Mam, red-eyed and exhausted, woke John and said, "Your father is dead." They cried while holding each other. His father had lived a hard life while farming for this large brood and sacrificing his first love—school. Now, however, he had eternal peace. They both went in to see Daniel, console him, and bring him into the kitchen near the fire.

Preparations began for Da's wake, which, of course, would be held in their home. Mam washed the body and dressed Da in his suit and a fresh white shirt. His body was placed in the parlor, where mourners would be free to say a prayer for his soul. Delicious dishes of chicken, fish, potatoes, carrots, and cabbage were carefully cooked and arranged for the wake. It was very important to honor their father. Finally, the house was cleaned from top to bottom. Mam's sister, Phyllis, arrived with her family and many meals. It was such a comfort for Mam to have another adult supporting her. Many friends and neighbors also made the long journey to their home and brought kind words and sympathy. They all shared heartwarming memories of Da. Their company provided a distraction for the entire family so that life seemed a trifle easier for the moment. And then Daniel died.

Chapter 2

Moving Forward

Puck Fair

Losing Da and Daniel was a disaster for Mam and her children. Although they were aware of the prognosis early on, the reality was so much worse. The loss of two family members left a huge void in their lives, an unending sadness. They loved their father, who had great expectations for his children and had encouraged them in so many ways. Da farmed the same land that his ancestors had worked since the late seventeenth century. He had shared this history often to make his family members proud of their roots, the farm, and the profession. It gave them a purpose and kept them alive. Now the farming was up to them, even though they were young. Life in Eskadour would never be the same.

Despite their mourning, somehow, Mam was able to reassure each of her children about the future. Some needed more attention than others did, but Helena O'Sullivan Lyne intuitively provided that nurturing. She prided herself on the strong family bond that enveloped her children and prayed it would survive the test. They had to rely on each other to get the job done. She often spoke of Da and Daniel, especially the things Da taught them and Daniel's sense of humor. Though gone, their spirits would remain with the children always. Her great faith assured her of their eventual reunion in heaven, but even in the present, she managed to make Da and Daniel's memories so vivid that the children saw them as a lasting force in their world. This was her vision:

> They shall be remembered forever,
>
> They shall be alive forever,
>
> They shall be speaking forever. (Yeats and Gregory 1907)

Over time, Mam was able to soothe their hearts, assuage their grief, and return humor and joy to their lives. The younger children still attended school and helped on the farm when they returned home. With a modicum of peace restored to their souls, life returned to a new normal. Though the sorrow remained, it softened, faded, and eventually morphed into happy memories. Margaret and Mary had finished school and helped Mam around the house and with the younger children. The work was unending and exhausting. Just fetching the water was a major chore because it was not in an easily accessible place.

Nevertheless, they pursued their chores bravely and attempted to help Mam with the farm, but eventually Mam and some of the children realized that it wasn't enough. Richard, who was now the oldest boy, stayed home from school when it was time to cut the hay or plant the potatoes, but he tried to go as often as possible. By spring, Mam knew that more hands were needed, so John also joined his brother in maintaining the farm.

Despite their father's hope for their future education, Richard and John left school within a year. It was a shocking reality at first, but ultimately a necessity. With so many demands on their time, school was now a luxury. John and Richard became farmers and assisted their mother. They graduated from collecting the eggs to shearing the sheep and cutting their own peat. They had learned many of these skills by observing Da since they were four years old. Now, however, it was their responsibility. John knew how Da had felt about education and how distasteful this choice would have been to him, but there was no alternative. Mam could not do it alone.

As the boys faced their new responsibilities, they were focused and determined. Each evening after dinner, they sat next to Mam and planned the next day's tasks. Tools were put at the ready if more peat was necessary. If planting must begin or the sheep had to be sheared, they decided in the evening how to manage it. Could the two boys complete the job themselves or should all three attempt it together? If a solution could not be found, they visited a neighbor and soon found a resolution. Within a few years, Jeremiah joined them, so the farm became more manageable.

Meanwhile, the older girls helped to care for the youngest children, Christopher and Nora and helped to prepare the meals, milk the cows, and feed the animals. For the most part, it ran well. If an occasional problem arose, they all tackled it until it was remedied. On occasion, a neighbor would stop by to provide advice or a helping hand. As the years went by, their skills improved, and their new roles became part of them.

One chief source of joy for the young men during this time was the Puck Fair. It was a thrilling event for these young farmers and the height of the farming season. This festival had begun hundreds of years earlier in Killorglin, County Kerry. Some said that it had begun before Saint Patrick's arrival, but others told of a myth connected with the occasion. According to this story from the seventeenth century, a herd of goats managed to escape Cromwell's attacking forces. While most of the goats headed for the mountains, the male goat made its way back to Killorglin. The creature was so exhausted when it returned that the locals guessed it must have been running from the British army during the British Civil War. With this advance notice from the goat, the townspeople were able to prepare and defend themselves from this vicious oppressor, thus saving the town.

Of course, this story didn't quite match dates in history; however, there was another theory that the festival began with the Celtic pagan celebration of Lughnasa. Whatever its origin, the festival has had a very long history, which honored a goat that was captured and crowned each year. The Irish word for *goat* is *poc*, which eventually evolved into Puck Fair to honor the goat that saved so many lives. During the well-attended three-day August festival, farmers bought and sold horses, cattle, and sheep. Many vendors were also there to sell their wares (Blackwell 2004).

John loved the festival more every year. He was very fond of all the animals on the farm and recognized their kind natures. Richard and Jeremiah felt the same way. This day provided a display of many creatures. The horses and other animals were sold on the first day, and the boys loved observing them as they were marched through the town by proud owners who were forced to sell them to survive. Of course, the fun of being with so many young people may have been another incentive.

As farmers, it was an important business day. The boys and Mam had decided exactly what had to be sold to keep the farm afloat. The money that was raised by selling one or two animals might get them through the next winter. The three of them negotiated earnestly for boys of their age. They usually made the money that was needed. But once business was finished, the young men had a grand time.

In 1921, they were really looking forward to joining in the festivities that took place on August 10, 11, and 12. Where else could you find a three-day fair? There were incredible crowds in the tiny town. Besides the buying and selling of animals, singers and musicians lined the streets and entertained. Once they arrived in Killorglin, they were fascinated by the throngs of people who were milling about and by the almost palpable excitement in the air. They were mere spectators most of Gathering Day, but later in the day they proceeded with Mam's plan to sell two sheep to help them get through the winter. Then they could enjoy the rest of the fair with their friends. Within hours, they were able to sell the sheep, which had been fattened up during the previous month. They negotiated an excellent price, and they were totally delighted with themselves. John stuffed the money in a small pouch and placed it securely in his pocket. They were off.

Immediately, they found several young men from nearby farms, and together they investigated all that the fair had to offer. Their first stop was the goat. Wearing its crown, the King Puck goat was standing on a raised platform that overlooked the day's activities. Some observers were feeding him while others just laughed at the poor creature tied to a pillar. The boys then moved to a singer who was attracting a good deal of attention. Michael, a young outspoken friend of theirs, quietly commented, "The poor old guy sounds like a frog."

To which Richard added, "Do frogs sing off-key too?" Laughing, they moved through the town, said hello to neighbors, and shared opinions on the best-looking girls. Since they no longer attended school, young people outside of their family rarely appeared in their everyday lives. This explosion of youth was mesmerizing, and they delighted in every new face that passed by. The fair was a great celebration, and the glorious day made it very comfortable.

By late afternoon on the third day of the fair, they knew it was time to head home and show Mam how well they had done. The sheep were sold at a better-than-fair price. Delighted with their success, John reached into his back pocket for the money, but it wasn't there. At first, he believed his brother Richard was trying to trick him. In a half-joking tone, he turned to Richard and asked, "Did you take the money from my pocket?"

"I haven't touched that money! Did you lose it, John?" Richard asked. The brothers stared at each other for a long, tense moment. This pouch of money would help pay their bills for a few months. Not having it was unthinkable! Mam would be so disappointed, and how would they cope? Would they lose the farm? (This was a thought that had lingered in their home since their father's death.) Would they be the cause of the family's final destruction?

John ran to the top of the street where they had spent so many hours over the past few days. Richard and Jeremiah followed quickly behind him. Standing at the main intersection, they surveyed the area, gazed at the crowd, and assessed each person who walked by. Then they moved into the crowd. Many vendors were still hoping to sell their wares, although the crowd was thinning.

They passed by a group of young men who were laughing and pointing at the poor old goat. Eyeing them suspiciously, they remained on the periphery to see if there were any unusual behaviors. Eventually, Richard gave up. As he turned, he noticed a strangely dressed man at the pottery table, just twenty feet away. He was haggling with the vendor and trying to get the price of a set of pottery reduced. Their voices sounded angry.

The vendor finally conceded, and the strange man reached for his money. Richard was shocked when he saw that the purse the strange man pulled out of his pocket was John's pouch. His immediate reaction was to grab the man and hit him until he returned the pouch. John heard the scuffle, and he and Jeremiah ran to help their brother. At the same time, the vendor was trying to defend the strange man, who might have been his final sale at the fair.

Richard screamed, "John, John, he has the money! Help me! Grab him!" And John did. Just then, a farmer, who had been packing up his pigs for the day, glanced quickly to see the cause of all the noise. Those seconds of inattention allowed his pigs to run for the hills as they squealed. They rushed in several directions, escaped their owner, and added to the chaos. By this time, many others had also taken notice. A small crowd had gathered. They observed the fight and tried to avoid the pigs.

The thief pushed Richard out of the way and yelled, "These boys are trying to rob me!" Many people in the crowd believed him and grabbed the boys with the assistance of the vendor, who wanted to be paid.

John couldn't believe this man might get the money. He said to the crowd, "If this is his money, he should be able to tell us what the pouch contains." Many of the onlookers stopped to consider the boy's comment. They agreed it was a sensible idea. Fortunately, the *garda* (police officer) had heard the crowd's cheering and raced to the scene. He arrived in time to hear John's suggestion. After hearing several versions of the fight, he secretly queried the boy on the other contents and agreed that the stranger should be aware of the other contents.

The thief tried to get out of answering, but the garda held firm and said, "Due to the poor harvests of the last few years, every man here can tell you the exact amount of money he's carrying. If this is yours," he said, holding the pouch aloft, "in addition to the money, what else does it contain?"

The thief muttered, "There's nothing else in that pouch but my money."

The garda checked the pouch and planned to tell the crowd the contents, but before he could, Richard yelled out, "A Saint Brendan medal is pinned to the inside." Mam relied on Saint Brendan, the patron saint of Kerry, and often kept his medal next to things of importance.

The garda smiled and nodded in agreement. He handed the pouch to the boys, grabbed the thief, faced the crowd, and said, "This thief is coming with me." The crowd cheered as the garda led the thief away. Delighted with their win, the boys congratulated each other and enjoyed the cheers for their victory. Richard took the pouch and placed it carefully in his pocket. The Lyne farm was saved for one more year.

Chapter 3

Margaret and Mary Leave Home

Mam was concerned about their many financial problems and was coming to the realization that selling a few animals each year, and the wool from the sheep wouldn't provide enough financial support. What was the alternative? Although the older children had assisted their mother with the farming and caring for the youngest children, the family still struggled to feed and clothe the twelve people in the house. There had to be another source of income in order to survive.

Mam's sister, Sarah O'Sullivan Donnelly, who lived in the States, had written many times and asked the older girls to come to America while singing its praises. John heard Sarah's explanation that many jobs were available in Rhode Island, where she lived. Irish people were arriving all the time, but Mam had said that the girls were too young. It was painful to watch her face this dilemma. Could she send them off to America alone to face God knows what? On the other hand, their income could change the lives of those who stayed behind in Ireland. The benefits were endless: fewer mouths to feed and a steady income since the girls would send money home. John was aware that Mam was trying to give this some serious consideration, but the outcome might break her heart.

There were additional problems in Ireland. The crops in many western counties were not doing well. This caused problems and even starvation for some. There was also major political strife during this era. Ireland had undergone great changes since John's encounter with the Black and Tans. Most of Ireland was independent, an incredible feat, but unfortunately, not all Irishmen felt the agreement was acceptable. According to the Anglo-Irish Treaty of 1921, the country was divided in two. Northern Ireland was under the control of the British king. An independent Republic of Ireland included twenty-six of the thirty-two counties. Because of strong feelings on both sides, a civil war began. Fighting continued, and blood was shed throughout the Emerald Isle. These were difficult times in many ways. The fighting began among former friends. Members of the Irish Republican Army (IRA) were on both sides of the treaty. Peace was lost again. Eventually, the treaty passed but not the division.

Despite all this national fighting, the Lyne family could not focus on political events while they were dealing with survival. Yes, the fighting between factions was awful but how could they feed all these children? How could they solve their financial problems? There seemed to be only one solution—emigration.

Because emigrating had become a popular topic among girls their age, Margaret and Mary were able to pick up a good bit of information from friends and neighbors. The price of a ticket to America was five pounds each, which was quite expensive for the family. Could Mam spare that much for the two of them to go together? John often overheard these tense conversations and recognized that Mam, Margaret, and Mary had the family's welfare at heart. As frightening and lonely as it felt to think of leaving home, they recognized the opportunity it would provide for those who were left behind. Nervous about asking Mam for the fare, they dropped the topic and prayed, which renewed peace in their household for a time. They continued to make bread, clean the potatoes and vegetables, and take care of the youngest children. They tended the garden when time allowed and completed many other household chores. The other children hoped for the best.

The discussions may have ceased, but Mam, Margaret, and Mary couldn't stop thinking about America. Was it the answer or the problem? Within a month, Aunt Sarah wrote again. They presumed she was just inquiring if any minds had changed about their trip. Mam gathered her children around her to share the latest letter. John sat next to Mam in support. She tore the letter open while they awaited their aunt's greetings, but something fell to the floor before Mam could say a word: two prepaid tickets to New York. What an extravagant gift! It was very generous, yet it made the girls' leaving so real. Mam read the letter, and she and the girls cried. In fact, the entire family cried, although the youngest did not know why.

Once some kind of peace had been restored, Margaret, Mary, and Mam slipped into another room. They had to face the situation despite what was in their hearts. Mam said, "I know this is a wonderful opportunity for you, but I can't imagine this house without my two oldest girls." They all held hands as they spoke.

Margaret responded, "A chance to go to the States is grand, but in addition, the money we can earn could make a real difference here, Mam." Mary agreed, and they both waited for Mam's reaction. She looked at them, nodded her head, and hugged her girls. The decision was made. A date was decided for their departure.

When the remaining children heard, their reactions varied. John was especially wounded. He asked his brothers, "What will we do without Margaret and Mary? Who will help prepare the dinner?"

Philip agreed and added, "Who will help Mam with the kids and the chickens?"

Michael quickly responded, "We will. Mam can't do it alone. There'll be more work than ever." Many of the younger members of the family only saw their own losses and not Mam's, Margaret's, or Mary's. They cared about them, but their youth limited their understanding of the lonesome, heart-wrenching separation that these three women would have to endure. The family had succeeded for years by stepping in and offering help wherever possible. They would miss their sisters, but only later, recognize the incredible loss.

Meanwhile, Mary and Margaret began preparing for their trip to America. They gathered their things, although there was little to get together, and decided when to book their trip. Their ship would depart from Queenstown, County Cork, which was named after

Queen Victoria in 1849 but later renamed Cobh once Ireland gained its independence. In the evenings, the girls had long chats about their futures and the people from Kerry who lived in America. Mary asked Margaret, "Do you think Aunt Sarah will be like Mam?"

Margaret was silent for a moment before responding. "Aunt Sarah may look like Mam, but it will never be the same. She has been very generous by buying us tickets, but we'll be lonesome."

"I'll miss everyone. Do you think we'll ever be back?" Mary asked.

Margaret quickly replied, "I couldn't leave if I believed I'd never be back. We'll return, Mary. You'll see." The farm had been their lives, and now they were facing a new world. God would help them. These conversations never included their mother because they wanted to avoid upsetting her.

Mam had many silent moments as she envisioned Eskadour without Margaret and Mary. It wasn't just their help that she enjoyed but their company. It was so wonderful to be able to discuss her plans with these very able, independent young women. Life was going to change for all involved. The less that was said, the better.

Their day of departure finally arrived. Wearing their best dresses, the girls carried their bags into the kitchen, where all eyes focused on them. They looked lovely to their younger sisters Lena, Sheila, and Nora as they observed their big sisters parade by. If it had been a dance, they would have been delighted to admire them, but this was so much more. Was it the last meeting? And then they had to face Mam, the woman who had brought them through the loss of their Da and Daniel, soothed their broken hearts, kept them together, and managed a big farm as well. Despite the terrible pain, she hugged her girls without tears, told them to write as often as they could, picked up one of their bags, and headed outside to Mike O'Shea's horse and buggy. The others followed close behind her, trying to hide their feelings and bid a final goodbye to their oldest siblings. O'Shea would take them to town to meet the train. The girls glanced at the farm and their brothers and sisters one last time and hopped into the buggy.

Mike tried to hold a conversation with them, but the girls were so lost in their own sorrow that they could barely speak. Despite Margaret's brave words, it was terrifying to accept the enormity of the moment that would stay with her for a lifetime. Mary held her hand as they watched the horse trot along. After several hours, they arrived at the train that would take them to Cobh.

The crowd in town wasn't especially large, but the train was already full. Once they boarded, the search for a seat began. As they eyed each compartment very carefully, they found no seats, but they did discover some interesting passengers. One family, with seven children, occupied a mere four seats. The children squeezed as close as possible to their parents in each chair. As they stepped into the next passenger car, they noticed an elderly gentleman resting on a tattered suitcase and chatting with a little boy while the rest of the family looked on approvingly.

The sisters patiently waited for their stop. It was the same place where most of the passengers would disembark. Although they were hours ahead of schedule to board their ship, they were pleased to get off the train and find a place to sit. They were a little calmer now. They chatted easily about family and the way each person had reacted as they had said goodbye. Margaret noticed the way Mam had been so stoic, to set an example for the rest. Compelled to remain strong, Mam knew this event would be repeated often in her lifetime. On the other hand, Lena and John, who had always been the most sensitive members of the family, had not been able to control their tears. The youngest children, Chris and Nora, were visibly upset too.

In Cobh, Mary and Margaret took a stroll along the harbor and stopped to view the ship, the *Baltic*, which would take them to America. It was enormous and took up a good part of the harbor. Traveling on this ship seemed so grand. The more they viewed it, the more excited they became. Margaret took out their tickets to check the time and date, May 8, 1922. Soon, they would be sailing into New York Harbor, where they would meet Aunt Sarah for the first time. Together, they would take the train to Providence, Rhode Island. They noted this new place and hoped it would be everything that they had heard about America.

After what seemed like an eternity but was probably three or four hours, the harbor began to awaken, and the crowd shifted in the direction of the ship. Some passengers even began to board the ship once it became clear that it was ready for business. Tickets were checked each time someone reached the gangplank, and the sailor in charge directed each guest to the appropriate level.

Mary and Margaret had gotten in line early because they had arrived at the harbor so many hours beforehand. Although they were still saddened by their goodbyes and leaving Ireland, Mary realized that the ship would take them on a fabulous trip across the ocean. Then the sailor in charge directed them to the lower deck—steerage. After a few glimpses of the rest of the ship, their accommodations were disappointing. They were directed to a very large room that had many berths. They chose two beds next to each other, which were covered by blankets. The ship had also provided a washbasin and a towel with each berth. A dinner of boiled fish or meat, potatoes, and black bread was served on long tables with benches in one of the unoccupied steerage accommodations. Although they had heard stories about the ships to America, they had hoped for more. Some noisy groups sang songs occasionally, while others who traveled with larger groups chatted about their futures. The girls were quiet around others, and only spoke to each other.

In a kind of whispered sigh, Mary said, "I guess this is it."

Margaret looked at her sister and said, "We saw how strong Mam was when we left the house. She refused to cry or express her fears. You know she held her feelings in to show all of us how to deal with difficulty. Well, Mary, this is our difficulty, and by sticking together, we can do it." With that attitude, the girls made it through the voyage, despite the food, conditions, and crowd.

Nine days later, when they arrived in New York, the excitement on board was fierce. All the passengers were anxious to see New York for themselves. The girls wanted to see their Aunt Sarah and to be free of the *Baltic*, but before they could leave, everyone in steerage was ferried to Ellis Island for a medical and legal inspection. Names were checked against the manifest. A superficial check for unusual rashes or body deformities took place. The girls had no problems, but the entire process took four hours. They were concerned about their aunt waiting so long. They waited in line after line, for someone's approval, as time dragged on and on. When they finally stepped on land in New York, they feared that their aunt may have lost faith in their arrival, but then a face very similar to their mother's suddenly appeared. It was Aunt Sarah. She held her arms open wide and welcomed them to America.

Chapter 4

Tim Dolan's Wake

As Margaret and Mary worked in Providence, Rhode Island, that year, life in Eskadour improved. Like many Irish immigrants, the girls faithfully sent half their pay back to Ireland. Those back home gradually felt the change in many ways, but most of all, Mam could relax and stop worrying about losing the farm. The rest of the family enjoyed an easier life. In fact, John and his friends had occasions when life became very interesting.

One Sunday in their local church, John was seated directly behind his good friend Michael Timmons. He noticed Michael's discomfort in his stiff Sunday attire as he ignored his parents and siblings, who were sitting alongside him. Instead, Mike was totally focused on each new arrival, especially any pretty girl that walked down the aisle. In less than two minutes, one girl named Mary Sheehan had his complete attention. She was sitting just across the aisle from him. His body might have been required by the church and his parents, but they couldn't control his mind. Mike even considered leaving his seat to speak to Mary, but the mass was just about to begin.

Mike's family observed his wandering eyes and whispered something in his ear, just as the priest emerged from the sacristy. He faced the altar and assumed a much more serious air. From that point on, the atmosphere became solemn, even though Mike was not completely absorbed in the spirituality of the moment. However, he did listen as the names of the deceased were being read. Among those mentioned was a neighbor, Tim Dolan. Shocked, Mike repeated the announcement to his brother, "Tim Dolan is dead!" This farming community knew the Dolan clan very well because the family had owned land in this part of Kerry for more than two hundred years. Tim had suffered so much from his many years of plowing and planting that he had developed a hump on his back, which had often aggravated his breathing. Just months earlier, many people in the town had celebrated his eighty-fifth birthday at Smith's pub. That was when Mike and his friends—John, Miles, and Philip—really became acquainted with the old man.

They still recalled some of their neighbors' antics during the night of his birthday. Mary Dowd's singing caused more than one dog in the vicinity to howl. Several gentlemen attempted to harmonize with two tone-deaf participants. Even Dolan joined in the festivities, reciting with great relish,

> Wine comes in at the mouth
> And love comes in at the eye;
> That's all we shall know for truth
> Before we grow old and die.
> I lift the glass to my mouth,
> I look at you, and I sigh. (Yeats 1989)

Yes, it was a great night, and the boys got a kick out of Tim.

Of course, once he died, a wake was immediately planned at his home, as was customary. A very large turnout was expected. In preparation, family members cooked a variety of dishes to feed the crowd, and beverages of all kinds were at the ready. Despite their sorrow in losing this kind man, many looked forward to recalling his life with friends and neighbors. The boys, however, weren't terribly enthused about attending the wake. At fifteen, these final tributes certainly did not stir their interests. But it was 1925 and burying the dead—a corporal work of mercy—was a well-respected tradition in Catholic Ireland. Their presence was expected. So early that evening, the boys met on the Coast Road and made their way to Dolan's wake. Mike, the most outspoken boy, led the way while John, Philip, and Miles followed.

As the boys proceeded to the Dolan's homestead, they considered ways to make this evening slightly more entertaining. Miles asked, "Should we steal a bottle from their house and save it for tonight?" The boys all agreed that it made sense but that it might be difficult with so many parents present.

"Some of the best-looking girls around will be at the wake. This could end up being a great night," Miles observed. A few female names were mentioned, but each of the girls would probably arrive escorted by a parent.

Discouraged, the group grew rather quiet until Mike said, "Mr. Dolan had a terrible hump on his back. I wonder how the family can make his body lie flat in the coffin for the wake."

Philip reacted immediately, saying, "They might break the bone in his back."

"Oh, no," John yelled. "Why would they do a thing like that?"

"It's not so bad," Mike replied. "He's dead anyway. You can't hurt him, and he will appear more presentable."

"For God's sake," John blurted. "Have you no respect? It's enough he's dead. Does he have to look good too?" The boys laughed at John's sensitive response and continued their discussion as they walked toward their destination. Mr. Dolan's hump inspired a variety of solutions.

Ultimately, Philip said, "His family has lived with this possibility for many years. They probably had an answer long before now." Even though Philip thought his final remark would conclude the conversation, Mike was not satisfied. He just had to offer one more idea.

"Maybe they just tied him in place to look presentable and to avoid an ugly bone-breaking scene." This idea certainly seemed more plausible, and they discussed how they would do it. Mike went on to explain, "They could cut holes in the bottom of the casket beneath the finished padding, tie a rope under the old man's shirt, and then secure it with a strong knot." Each of them offered suggestions to make the process easier until they were satisfied that it could be done well. During the final quarter mile of their journey, they moved on to more interesting topics, such as the food that young Mrs. Dolan, Austin's wife, may have prepared.

As the house came into view, they were impressed by the number of people who had come to say farewell. Many boys their own age had arrived with their parents, but several stragglers joined their little group. They all made their way through the crowd and approached the front door together. The first thing that John noticed was the vast amount of food set out in the kitchen and the number of people surrounding the table. If they wanted to get to the food before it was devoured, they had better move fast. They spoke quickly to several family members, expressing their grief and praising Dolan and his many accomplishments. Then, because they were aware of the many people ahead of them, they joined the line for dinner. Gradually, they reached the overflowing offerings of sliced ham, freshly cooked chicken, potatoes floating in butter, fresh vegetables, soda bread, and as expected, a bit of tea. Abandoning any semblance of decorum, the boys dove in, filled their plates, and settled in a corner to taste their delicious findings. Once they had their fill, the conversation resumed among the four young men.

"Are you ready to get a look at the old man?" Mike asked John, Philip, and Miles.

"We'll have to join them in the parlor for that. Let's be very careful about the way we approach the casket, or it could cause trouble," John replied. Presuming they appeared quite casual, the group arose as one and slowly walked toward the parlor.

Austin, Mr. Dolan's son, stopped them, and they nervously awaited his comments. "It's heartwarming to see such young men willing to share our grief," he said, shaking hands with each of them. "God knows it was tough to lose Da, but to have so many pay their respects brightens our spirits." Guilt over their planned investigation made it difficult to look him in the eye. "Are you going in to say a prayer now?" he inquired. They nodded, smiled weakly, and uttered a few sounds in agreement. He stepped aside, and they proceeded with a much quicker pace to the parlor, where very few people remained. Most of the crowd was in the kitchen or near the fire, enjoying the food.

Aware of the other mourners, the boys stepped discreetly closer to the casket and knelt to say a prayer. Each boy took his time while observing Tim's clothes, the Bible lying next to him, and the rosary beads entwined in his fingers. They focused on the perimeter of his body, but of course, they dare not touch the corpse itself. After they had taken a turn examining the situation under the guise of saying a prayer, they sat near the casket and discussed their findings in whispers.

Mike noticed that Tim's body was lying totally flat, as if the hump had never existed. He told the other boys, "There's no sign of a rope." The others confirmed his findings but wondered if it could have been rigged out of the viewing public's sight.

"If there's no rope," Philip reasoned, "they must have broken his bones." The others winced at the idea. The conversation continued for a while at a fair distance from the other mourners.

Eventually, those remaining in the parlor left, and John, who had obviously given this a good deal of thought, announced, "There's only one way to find out. One of us must go under the casket and investigate the interior from the side near the wall. Only then will we know if a rope is tying the body down." The boys couldn't believe John's change of heart. In earlier discussions, John had been annoyed at the prospect of disrespecting the old man. Now, he was anxious to go to any extreme to discover how this was handled. Responding to their amazement, John said, "Well, if we plan to pursue this to the end, we have to find out the facts." Mike picked up on the idea immediately. Even though they had reservations, they agreed to investigate, especially now that they were alone in the parlor. The question was who would actually crawl beneath the casket. Fear of terrible consequences made them hesitant about taking such a risk. There would be hell to pay if they were discovered.

After all the pros and cons were presented, Mike finally acquiesced and immediately went into action. He slipped under the lace cloth that covered the empty space under the casket and slowly crawled to the wall behind it. John, the lookout, kept his eye on the door for intruders. Anxious but still in control, they awaited Mike's reappearance. To their surprise, a new group of mourners entered the parlor just a few minutes later, making the situation much more complicated. The other boys darted glances at each other, feared the worst, and prayed for an out. Unnerved by the pressure, John tapped on the casket to warn Mike, but there was no response. In this very tense moment, Tim's body moved. At first, it was almost imperceptible, but then his head rose six inches. The newcomers shrieked, and those in the kitchen came running in. Chaos broke out as the family reacted to the yells and rushed to the casket. One mourner blurted out, "Is he dead or not?" While witnessing this unholy mess, the boys were torn between Mike's terrible predicament and the fear of being caught. Ultimately, they dashed out the door, saving themselves and leaving Mike alone and hidden.

Austin Dolan, the deceased's son, tried to calm his guests. He suggested that everyone return to the kitchen and have a sweet while the family examined the corpse. The crowd, however, would not be silenced so easily. They returned to the kitchen and continued their own discussion. An older woman, looking at the group assembled in the kitchen, wondered aloud, "Do you think it could be the devil?" A silence fell over the mourners since her words revealed many of their thoughts.

Unshaken by this comment, the gentleman to her right responded in a very self-righteous tone, "Why would there be evil spirits in the home of a God-fearing Catholic man?" Now that the worst had been uttered, everyone abandoned propriety. A variety of superstitious myths reared their ugly heads.

"Was the window opened for his spirit to leave?" an old woman remarked.

Then a distant neighbor chimed in, "Did someone sit with the body all night to protect it?" No one felt compelled to suppress a thought. The exchange became so heated that they almost forgot about the household members who were trying to explain these strange occurrences to each other.

Eventually, the family deliberations in the parlor ended, and they quietly joined the others in the kitchen. Embarrassed, Austin revealed that they had used a rope to make their father's body lie flat. Somehow, it must have loosened, allowing his posture to return to its normal curve and pushing the head up. The mourners were all sympathetic, not to mention relieved. The talk of evil spirits seemed silly after this practical explanation, so the relieved mourners enjoyed the remaining refreshments and relaxed into chatty little groups. Everyone's tone had changed. They were unaware of the young man who was still concealed under the coffin.

Once quiet had been restored in the parlor, Mike waited to assure his safety. Finally, he very carefully peeked out from under the lace that surrounded the bottom of the casket to be sure that he was alone. At first, he was delighted to see an empty room, and he quickly slid from beneath the casket. Then he wondered about his friends. *Have they left? Have they abandoned me to bear the consequences alone?* He could hear the rest of the mourners talking in the kitchen, but he knew it was best to avoid that crowd, due to the scene he had just caused. He wondered how he could get out and avoid the others in the house. He couldn't exit through the front door with all the mourners just a few feet away, so he tried the windows, which proved impossible to open. Using a key, he scraped at the paint that had sealed a window closed. He perspired as he overheard the conversation coming from the kitchen. Wiping the sweat from his brow, he finally succeeded in forcing the window open. Pleased with himself, he climbed onto the sill and jumped to freedom. To his surprise, his pals had been waiting for him all along. They softly called to him as soon as he hit the ground. Somewhat ashamed of leaving Mike to his own devices but more curious about the outcome, they pulled him to the back of the house and pummeled him with questions. "Were you frightened? Was there a rope? Why did you make Tim's body jump?"

Happy to be back with his friends, Mike took a breath and told them exactly what had happened. "I was looking at the bottom of the casket and found the rope right away. Our theory was correct. They chose to tie him down rather than break a bone."

"Right, right, but why did you make his body move?" Philip inquired.

"As I was assessing the kind of knot they used, I heard other voices. I was so scared that I accidentally pulled one end. I couldn't believe the result."

"You were shocked? You should have seen the faces of the family," John calmly observed.

Mike could barely control his laughter, although he kept a watchful eye on the Dolan's house in case a member of the family appeared. Mike went on to explain, "I could hear them talking when they gathered around the casket. Thank God, they blamed Austin, Dolan's oldest son, for tying such a pitiful knot. They called him an "eejit" (idiot), saying he caused the whole embarrassing episode. He was chosen to explain the incident to the crowd, God help him." They all had a good laugh at Austin's hopeless state. Mike added, "Once they decided he was the culprit, they didn't even bother to try to adjust the old man. They merely closed the casket and left the room."

Astonished and grateful for their good luck, the young men walked toward the path as they relived every delicious moment of the evening. This was definitely the wake of a lifetime.

Chapter 5

John Plans to Leave Eskadour

Several years had passed since Mary and Margaret's departure. Life in Eskadour had a calmer, easier atmosphere. The girls, who were now in their midtwenties, continued to send money home every month. Mam missed them and read their letters aloud to all the siblings, who listened excitedly to their adventures. They had moved to New York City, where many Irish immigrants had settled, some from Kerry. The streets of New York were busy and filled with a variety of accents. They also found some unusual styles there, such as flapper dresses and women wearing very short hair, but all in all, they were having a grand time with their new friends at dances and traveling in the city. The children loved all their stories, especially since Mam was so relaxed as she read their letters, which demonstrated how her daughters were thriving. The family was much more comfortable now that Margaret and Mary sent home money, so life had definitely improved.

Positions in their household continued to change. In addition to the girls leaving, the youngest children, Chris and Nora, were now ten and twelve, so they could also contribute some help on the farm. They took care of the chickens and eggs and cleaned the chicken coop before or after school. This was a duty that many siblings had shared and the first step in assuming responsibility on the farm. Sheila took over the vegetable garden and helped with the farm. Lena left home for America about a year after her older sisters. Thus, the number at home had decreased to nine, including Mam. Three were gone and sending part of their paychecks home. The duties on the farm had also shifted. It became too much for Mam to work the farm and take care of the house, so Richard, Jeremiah, John, and the twins, Michael and Philip worked the farm; however, they were still under Mam's supervision. Things were running smoothly, but opportunities beyond farming were scarce. Searching for a position was fruitless because so many young people from large families were seeking the same jobs. John was eighteen and thinking about a future outside of Kerry or even Ireland. The trouble was that he had become Mam's right hand and helped her with many responsibilities beyond the farm.

Mam's sister Phyllis lived several miles away. Because Mam enjoyed visiting her sister occasionally, John felt that it was his responsibility to escort her the three miles, which she would have walked alone. With a very old-fashioned and respectful attitude, he waited outside while the two women enjoyed a lively conversation over tea. They shared secrets and solved or at least sympathized with each other's problems. They needed that time to themselves. The one luxury that he could give her was time for her to speak to a trusted sister about her concerns and plans. John had become a real farmer and checked Aunt Phyllis's animals as he waited for his mother. Sometimes he offered advice on a particular creature's needs, but most of the time, he was content to relax after a long day. Once the visit was over, he bid a fond goodbye to Aunt Phyllis, and he and Mam walked home as she shared some of the ladies' interesting chats.

But now it was time for John to leave. He couldn't see a future in Eskadour, so he wrote to his siblings in America about his plan. He wasn't quite ready to share this with Mam, so he confided in his sister Sheila, who agreed with his assessment but cautioned him to break the news slowly and carefully. John worked on the farm as usual and waited for the right moment. Jeremiah, Philip, and Michael helped him with the cows and sheep, but he remained nearby in case they needed assistance. He felt this was their training ground, preparing them to take over when the time was right. Richard, the strongest brother of all, planted the potatoes and cut the peat.

Sheila and John discussed his leaving whenever they had a moment to themselves, but he had to avoid being obvious. She was sorry to see her older brother planning his departure, but there seemed to be little choice. His plan took place slowly.

It seemed, however, that Sheila wasn't the only family member interested in John's plan. One spring evening after working in a distant field, John and Richard were slowly heading home, exhausted. Tired from such a long day, John could no longer keep his secret from Richard, and blurted out, "I'm leaving soon."

Richard turned and asked, "What are you talking about?"

"We bring in very little money on this farm, Richard. Margaret, Mary, and Lena are keeping us all alive. I want to contribute. Anyway, what future can we have here? I've written to Margaret and Mary, and they agree it's time for me to go to America. In a few months, they'll help me with the passage." During their entire conversation, Richard stood with his mouth open. The brothers had always been best of friends since they were only two years apart. This revelation was a total shock for Richard. He knew this startling news would change their lives.

He tried to argue, "Do you think you should make that trip alone, John?"

John was so focused that he couldn't bear any more changes to the plan and responded, "I've made up my mind. Next fall, I'm going." Even though Richard was upset, he remained silent.

As the spring concluded, the entire family was consumed with caring for the farm. The early potatoes had been harvested and stored. The sheep needed shearing, and a good deal of money could be gathered from the wool. The barn was kept meticulously clean, and the cows were tended to because the milk also produced an income. The family needed all the money that the farm could earn, so they all pitched in when and wherever they could help. When all was completed for the most part, it was again time for Puck Fair, which was a favorite for all of them. The plan was to spend a few hours at the fair whenever they could during the three days in Killorglin.

John finally had a chat with Mam about his plans. Of course, she was sad to hear that yet another one of her children planned to leave for America, but the others had done so well, and their letters were so cheerful that she was convinced New York was a grand place. There were loads of Irish people, plenty of jobs, and positive futures. Since Da's death, John had been very close to her. She would miss those chats in the evenings while they prepared for the next day's work, but her children had to find their own way.

The night before their first day at the fair, Mam complained of dizziness, which was very unusual for this strong woman. She attributed it to all the hustle and bustle on the farm during the previous month and assured them that it was nothing to worry about. Despite her persuasive powers, John and Sheila stayed home that afternoon, just to be sure. After their morning chores, the others headed for Puck Fair. Mam rested, which was a luxury for her. Later, the three had a cup of tea and talked for an hour. They avoided any difficult subjects like John's upcoming trip and instead spoke of plans for the farm, the three sisters in New York, and a neighbor's child leaving—anything that made Mam relax. Eventually, she began to doze, and gently, they escorted her to bed and tucked her in for the night.

There were still a few chores to complete, so Sheila and John finished up and returned home. A few hours later, everyone came back from the fair. They were eager to share all they had seen and done, but John quieted them, whispering, "Mam is sleeping soundly, so we must talk very quietly." They stepped outside to share their experiences and have a laugh or two. Then they returned to the house to sleep.

That night they were awakened by Mam's groans as she experienced terrible chest pains. They knew that she needed a doctor's care. Quickly, Richard and John went to a neighbor's house to borrow a horse and cart to bring her to the local doctor, Dr. O'Shea. He, too, was concerned about Mam's heart. He felt that she should be admitted to the hospital for observation until they could determine her precise problem.

Mam went to the hospital and remained there for eight days. Though they all took turns visiting to lift her spirits, they were very nervous about her condition. Mam was only in her late forties. They wondered if her heart could really be so vulnerable. While there, Mam wrote a letter to Sheila, instructing her to help John prepare for his trip. She wasn't sure how long she would be in the hospital, and she wanted him to be fully prepared with enough underwear and shirts to travel to the States. She also provided instructions for the day of the voyage.

Eventually, they released her with medication. Of course, they were all delighted to have her back home, but they remained cautious and watched her every step. They divided her chores among themselves so that she could rest as long as possible. However, Mam had a hard time letting go and tried to join in preparing dinner or mending whatever needed her sewing needle. It went against her nature to sit while everyone else was occupied. This went on for weeks until she finally felt like her old self.

She began joining in the daily chores slowly and on a limited basis. She said that she felt fine. Her children loved Mam returning to life and celebrated her improvement. As Mam's strength increased, she decided to join her sons in bringing the cows to market in Cork, which was quite a long walk. She was determined to be part of this regardless of all the warnings that had been issued by her family. That morning, she felt great and anxious to get started. The boys drove the cows down to the road, and they all set out for Cork. She did quite well for most of the trip, and when they stopped to have lunch, she seemed fit. As they passed a church in Castletownbeare, she stopped to say a prayer. Since she was always interested in saying a little prayer whenever possible, this was no surprise to her children. However, Mam took so long this time that Richard began to worry.

So Richard went searching for her, and found her dead on the church floor. Did she know this was the end of her life? Did she choose to be in a church when the time came? Whether she knew or not, it was a terrible blow for all of them. The woman who had spent the last ten years as father and mother to her children could not overcome her weakened heart. It took several days to accept the loss of their mom. It was especially shocking to the older ones, who recalled, all too well, the death of their father and the way their mother had held them together. Her supportive conversations and deep faith had convinced all of them that life would be much brighter in the future, that sorrow doesn't have to last forever, and that change can be tolerated and accepted. Now they quoted Mam in their explanations to the younger children when trying to provide comfort to them.

Mam's sister, Phyllis, and her daughters came immediately and offered great assistance. They helped arrange the wake for the family. Food was prepared, the church was contacted, and the dates were set aside. At twenty, Richard was the oldest sibling at home now, but he consulted with the others in making decisions. The three oldest sisters in New York were informed via a telegram—a message that changed their lives yet again. Margaret and Mary bought tickets for home.

Were the brothers remaining on the farm—Richard, John, Jeremiah, Michael, Philip, and the youngest, Chris—capable of maintaining this property? Could they survive without assistance? When Margaret and Mary arrived, these were the questions most often discussed. The older sisters felt that the youngest children could not stay, so they planned to bring Nora and Chris to New York. John was obliged to postpone his trip so they could reassess responsibilities on the farm. His plans were unknown by most of them. Despite all the preparation, the time was wrong. He had such a bond with Mam that her death had taken away any clear thinking. Sheila, who was only seventeen, would take on the motherly duties. And so, the arrangements were made. Now, in addition to their mother's death, they must say goodbye again to their eldest sisters and the youngest children in the family, Chris and Nora.

It seemed like a cloud hung over Eskadour for a long time. The young men continued to work hard, just as they had for Mam. They had taken on all the backbreaking work under their mother's supervision, so that part of their lives continued as usual. Mam had been the motivator, and she had made it quite clear that without their constant effort, the farm would not support their large family. The great change now was the loneliness. Sheila cooked and took care of the house, but they missed Mam enormously. Her singing and laughter had filled their lives. She had intervened in any sad moment and discussed any difficulty at length whenever one of them was in need. Her inspiration, great faith, and challenging words had lifted their spirits, and that strength remained a part of their lives forever. Failing her was unthinkable, so they followed in her strong, determined footsteps and strove to do their best.

Along with their own farm, the brothers occasionally worked for neighboring farmers to make ends meet. At times, they were exhausted, but it helped them all financially—a remnant of their mother's thinking. Everyone was up at the crack of dawn to begin each day. Right after breakfast, their individual chores began, and most of the brothers headed for the fields to plant, gather the hay, or do whatever the season demanded. One of them stayed behind with Sheila and assisted in the vegetable garden and with the chickens. They adapted to any unplanned needs, and things seemed to be running smoothly. For almost two years, they had manned the farm, respected each other, and often heard from their sisters in America, who questioned their efforts and encouraged each of them.

One morning, John took an early stroll to the mailbox and found a letter addressed to him from Margaret. He tore it open and read her reminder of his original plan to join them in New York. She repeated her invitation and mentioned the job opportunities in the city. "Despite the depression," she said, "there are still very optimistic attitudes among the Irish newcomers, so now is the time. Life in New York can only be easier than life in Ireland. Even if life in New York grows a little difficult, it will certainly pay better than the farm." John was surprised and delighted with the invitation, but he wondered if he could leave his brothers and sister? He knew they were functioning very well together without Mam, so maybe it was a possibility. He wavered as he considered his options and responsibility to his family. *Should I go?* Finally, he decided to ask for Sheila's advice once again.

The next morning, he rose before the rest and asked his sister to sit and have a small chat outside the hearing of the other siblings. They sat in a nook near the fireplace, and John began by telling her about his last letter. He told Sheila, "Margaret has asked me if I'm still interested in New York. Do you think it's too soon to think about leaving?"

Glancing at her brother and a little surprised, she said, "That's still on your mind, John?"

"I would have never stayed this long except for Mam's passing. My brothers have been at it for almost two years now without Mam and seem to handle the farm very well. Do you think they can do it without me?"

Sheila thought a minute and suggested, "To be honest, John, I'll miss you, but you seem determined, and Margaret thinks it's the right time. Get everything prepared for the trip. Check the dates of the ships leaving for New York, and when you're ready, we'll have this conversation again." Buoyed by Sheila's reaction, John left the kitchen in high spirits. He envisioned himself on the streets of New York and prayed that no disasters would befall the family again. He wrote to Margaret and told her that he was thinking of coming. He followed Sheila's advice and checked on the ships leaving for New York in the near future.

Two evenings later, while John sat in the kitchen reading the newspaper, Richard approached him and casually asked, "What are you up to, John?"

Hesitant but honest, John responded, "I'm checking the departure dates for ships to New York."

"So, you're thinking of going again?" Richard asked.

"I had always planned to go, and now that the farm is running so well, I think it's time," John answered.

"Well, I know you've made all the plans, but I'd really like to join you, John."

Now this could make a difference, John thought. Jeremiah, Michael, and Philip would have to work the farm alone. *Can they do it?* Sheila and John had another chat that evening. They considered all the positives and negatives. Richard was anxious to go to America and follow his dreams, but his brute strength would be missed on the farm. Nevertheless, Sheila thought he should go, and John was delighted to have his brother with him on the long journey.

They booked passage for the next month. The nearest date on the *Stuttgart* was September 7, 1930, almost a year after Black Thursday, the day the stock market in America had fallen and begun the Depression. Despite the stock market's crash, John planned to take the risk. Any job would be acceptable.

Telling the others was a difficult moment. They had all relied on each other more than ever since their mother's passing. John hated to disappoint them. Though he loved the farm, he didn't plan to be a farmer. Some of his brothers were more interested in it. They were all saddened by John's announcement that two more of their brothers were leaving, but those remaining were very good-natured in their response.

"You two do what you must do. We're fine here in Eskadour," said Jeremiah. John and Richard promised that a good part of their wages would return to Ireland every month. The matter was settled.

Now that it had all been discussed openly, John and Richard could share their thoughts about leaving. The two travelers received letters and tickets from their sisters, who were excited about their arrival. They all enjoyed hearing from their family in New York and loved all the enthusiasm surrounding this trip. In the interim, Margaret and Mary had married two Irishmen, John Nash and James Murphy, in addition to caring for the youngest members of the family. Things had changed in Ireland and New York, and now these two young men would see for themselves.

John still had the passport he had obtained for himself two years ago, but Richard had to get his. Once that was accomplished, they both packed their bags for the big day. Yes, they were excited to be heading for New York, but the night before they left, John kept thinking about the people they were leaving behind. Would he ever return to Ireland and see them again? He knew of so many people who had never returned! These same questions had haunted his sisters as they prepared to leave Ireland. The adventure of the trip and the sorrow for those left behind kept him awake the night before they left. He also wondered if he would find a job in New York City. There were so many questions and only hope for an answer.

A friend had promised to take them to Killarney. From there, they would take a train to Cobh, just as their sisters had. They rose early, gave hugs that lasted awhile, and went out the door, sad to leave but determined to succeed.

After a lengthy buggy ride to Killarney, they boarded the train to Cobh, where they met their German ship. For many European vessels, Cobh was the last stop before they crossed the Atlantic Ocean. Margaret had already warned them about steerage, so they weren't surprised as they boarded the ship. They found many young Irish and German people on board. Due to their love of music and John's outgoing nature, they felt right at home. The meals were plain and served on long tables, but the conversation, at least with their fellow Irish travelers, was consoling and often entertaining. The evenings passed with a variety of musicians playing songs as their fellow passengers sang along. In nine days, they landed in America.

John and Richard each had their own dreams, which they never shared. Each saw this as the beginning of his dream. This bustling city, which would one day be the source of their happiness, now seemed so foreign. When they landed, they saw a great number of people going about their business. Workers completed their jobs for the day, others met ships at the docks, and finally, the anxious passengers arrived alongside them. This was their first glimpse of America. The possibilities seemed endless because this was just the beginning.

Once they had gone through the processing center, Richard and John searched through the crowd that was waiting on the pier for the familiar faces of their sisters. They were not disappointed. Lena and Mary were thrilled to see how well these two looked after an additional two years of being responsible for the farm. Hugs and cheers were shared as they welcomed the new arrivals and headed for Margaret's apartment to have dinner. The big city was astonishing. It was noisy and crowded, but they were so caught up in their sisters' conversations that they barely had a chance to comment on the grandeur of New York City. They were now going to meet the two Irishmen their sisters had married, and this was only their first night in America.

While her sisters were down at the dock meeting the new arrivals, Margaret was home preparing a welcoming meal for her brothers. Once they arrived at Margaret's home, John and Richard greeted their sister and met Jack Nash, a charming man with a great sense of humor, who warmly welcomed these two Kerrymen. He, too, was born in Ireland, and he understood the shock and anxiety of viewing New York for the first time. They were also reunited with their brother Chris and sister Nora, who had changed somewhat after living in New York for two years. After a toast to the newcomers, they sat down to Margaret's delicious dinner. It was much finer than the fare they had been offered lately. After a long chat filling the Americans in on life in Ireland, the new arrivals were invited to stay at Mary's home. A short bus trip took them to her apartment, and they met Jim Murphy, a lovely, quiet man, who welcomed them into his home. That night, they slept like babies in Mary's living room, with John on the couch and Richard on a comfy easy chair.

In the morning, they would face the task of getting a job. For now, they had completed the voyage that would change their lives forever.

Part 2

Chapter 6

Terence McGovern

Thirty years earlier, in Cavan, Ireland, another family's son was trying to survive the nineteenth century. Terence McGovern loved Ireland and longed to become a farmer, but there was a problem. According to Irish custom, the eldest male inherited the farm, but unfortunately, Terence was not the oldest. Although quite young, he was determined to follow his dream, even if it seemed almost impossible. With few prospects available in Ireland at the end of the nineteenth century, Terence realized that he would have to leave Ireland to earn enough to buy a farm, so he planned to head for the States.

His brother Peter and sister Helen both lived in America and wrote home quite frequently, so he had a connection in New York. He wrote to tell them about his plan to sail to New York City and waited for their responses. Within a few weeks, they answered, and fortunately, Helen and Peter were delighted with Terence's plan. Helen wrote, "I'll be glad to see my baby brother here in the States with me." And they very generously included the price of his passage.

Once the good news arrived, Terence could think of nothing else, but it took him awhile to finally make the trip. Once he arrived in New York, he planned to get a job (after all the streets were lined with gold), work for a year or more, and return home to buy his own place. Youth and determination were on his side, and he felt that he had found the answer.

Although there was no guarantee of a job, Terence's optimism never wavered. He said goodbye to his parents and made his way south to Queenstown in Cork. Once aboard the ship, some of that enthusiasm wore a bit thin. It was a long, tiring voyage in steerage, and the close sleeping quarters bothered Terence more than he had expected. Working in open fields all his life had not prepared him for the claustrophobic atmosphere on the ship. When his ship docked, he was delighted to leave the tight space behind and search the crowd for his brother. But first, he had to make a quick stop at Ellis Island to verify his place of origin on the ship's manifest. It was quite easy to identify his brother because both men were quite tall and therefore, easy to spot in the overflowing crowd. Peter's warm greeting reassured Terence, and the two chatted happily as they hopped on a trolley and headed for Helen's apartment.

"You look well, Terence. How are the folks at home?" Peter inquired.

Terence tried to reply as gently as possible, "They're good, but it's hard for them watching us leave one at a time."

"But you'll be returning, Terence, right?" Peter wondered.

"I will once I earn enough money, but that may take a while. Any ideas for a job?"

"I just might have a few things in mind, boyo," Peter replied, and Terence was glad to hear it. They continued their route toward Helen's place. People on the streets were heading in many directions while the vendors were selling their wares. Terence found the crowds in New York distracting but the city was fascinating. He wondered if there was room for new arrivals. Despite the chaos, the trolley traveled quite easily with the two brothers sitting next to each other and commenting on all the sights. Terence was completely absorbed as he observed the streets of the city and asked his brother lots of questions as they passed by a long line of stores and buildings. Many children were playing on side streets. It was so different from what he was accustomed to in Ireland, but there was no doubt he was delighted to be there.

About thirty minutes later, Peter indicated that it was their stop, and both men stepped off the trolley and stood in front of Helen's apartment house. They climbed the steps in the courtyard and found her apartment on the second floor. As soon as they arrived at the front door, Terence was again warmly welcomed. Many years had passed since the three of them sat for a chat. As they talked in Helen's living room, the family's warmth was almost tangible. Helen had prepared a delicious meal, and the young men ate more than their fair share. Once they had relaxed on Helen's comfortable couch, Terence realized how tired he was. The ship had taken longer than expected, and although he had been thoroughly amazed by the look of the city and delighted to see his family, he could hardly stay awake. Helen made up the couch in the living room because there were no extra rooms in her small apartment. He was grateful just to lie down after his long adventure. Peter said his goodbyes and mentioned that he would return in the morning. Terence was asleep within minutes.

True to his word, Peter arrived the next morning at seven. He was delighted to wake Terence up and share his plans for the day. Peter had a friend in the ice business, and Terence might have a chance to get a job there. Terence was thrilled at the possibility, but he wondered if selling ice was steady work. Peter looked at his brother and said, "This man's been employed for years, so it seems pretty steady to me." Terence accepted the correction, dressed quickly, ate, and said goodbye to Helen. Peter rushed him out the door, and they joined the crowds of New Yorkers hurrying in every direction.

It was a cool autumn day when they took the trolley over to the Hudson. They put their collars up to protect them from the wind and headed downtown. Eventually, Peter indicated that they had found the right place. He stepped inside the door and left Terence on the sidewalk. Almost immediately, a man on the street approached Terence for some money, saying he was hungry. Although Terence was new to this country, he was not about to hand over the little money that he had. He suggested the fellow get a job. With a few unkind words, the beggar walked away, furious with this greenhorn.

Peter returned with his friend Joe and introduced him to Terence, his baby brother. When he repeated Terence's question about steady work, Joe was ready with a response. "Ice is big business in New York and all over America." He went on to tell Terence, "A very wealthy man named Charles Morse has considerable interest in this business and is frequently mentioned in the newspaper. Anyway, this man's firm, the

Consolidated Ice Company is growing and growing. He can always use some strong men on his payroll."

Of course, Terence was pleased and asked, "Is that the man we'll work for?"

Joe laughed and said, "We may be in the business, my boy, but we're on the local level." He went on to say, "My uncle has worked for the ice company for years, and he promised my brothers and me that we could get a job anytime."

Terence grew hopeful and asked, "Do you need to be a blood relative, or is any Irishman acceptable?"

Joe smiled and said, "Do you know anything about the business?"

Terence quite honestly confessed, "Not a thing."

"Come to work with me now, meet the boss, and we'll see how it goes." They all agreed and headed for the job. Joe was determined and enthused while Terence, though hopeful, was concerned. Once they arrived at the job, Joe went right to the boss and introduced Terence, who was a six-foot-two strapping young soul. All the men spoke for a few moments before the boss agreed that Terence should spend the day working with Joe. Terence was delighted to be given the opportunity. Peter was also happy for his baby brother, but he had to leave for his own job. Terence and Joe walked over to the stable where Joe greeted his horse with a treat. Terence wondered if New York might have more in common with Ireland than he thought. The horse was a reminder of home, and it provided a little more comfort in this strange new city.

Joe led the horse to another section of the business, and together, they harnessed the horse to the wagon. Once they climbed aboard, they went to fetch and load the ice, which was a backbreaking job. But with the two of them, the job was much easier.

Joe drove with a list of clients on the seat beside him. When they arrived at an apartment or business on the list, they quickly stepped down, and Joe showed Terence how to use the ice tongs to grab ahold of the ice block and then place it on his shoulder. Even with padding on his shoulder, the ice was heavy, cold, and uncomfortable, but Terence was able to manage it. Next, it was delivered to the customer and placed in the top of the icebox. Now that iceboxes were well-insulated, the ice blocks lasted longer, up to seven days. As they moved on, Terence was able to manipulate the tongs to gain a better hold. Joe and Terence finished their day and returned to the owner. With Joe's high praise, the job belonged to Terence, and he was thrilled. He expressed his gratitude and took his new friend out for a couple of beers to celebrate the occasion. Once he returned to Helen's, he wrote home sharing the good news. Life in New York City was grand.

The job was demanding. Lifting large pieces of ice and climbing all those stairs to ice boxes throughout the city took every bit of strength that Terence had, but it was reliable. He often started loading his cart for the day's deliveries at four in the morning and returned at five or six in the evening, exhausted. Helen provided a filling dinner, which he devoured in record time and frequently requested seconds.

Later he collapsed into bed. Terence was accustomed to working hard on the farm, so it was nothing new. On the other hand, his surroundings and the American lifestyle and accents were totally different here in New York. At times, so many living in such a small space was overwhelming, but he endured. Terence knew that all his adapting and hard work would help him reach his goal. The faster he earned enough for a farm, the sooner he would return to Ireland and buy his own place.

It took a little longer than he had planned, but two years later, Terence had enough for a farm and planned his return trip. Things were changing in the ice business, and Terence felt that he was leaving just in time. He wrote home letting them know that he planned to return. He bought his passage, quit his job, and thanked Helen, Peter, and Joe for their kindness. Although he appreciated all they had done for him, returning home had been his goal from the beginning. Now that it was finally time, he was delighted.

During his stay in New York, his mother had written about a farm that was being sold. He never mentioned it to anyone else but secretly hoped it was still available. As soon as he returned, he asked a good friend to accompany him to the farm for his first visit. They were both impressed with the place, which was just outside Bawnboy. In addition to a good-sized farm, there were several buildings on the property. Near the road, the property was protected by a large fence, which blocked the cows from wandering away. Thirty feet beyond the gate and to the left of the house stood a nice-sized henhouse. Twenty feet away, there was a rather new and somewhat roomy two-story whitewashed house.

When he stepped inside the door, he entered the main room, which had a settee and a big fireplace for cooking and warmth. Although it had a large table, a parlor in the next room could be used for finer dining. On the other side of the kitchen, there was a spacious bedroom. To the right of the front door, a narrow staircase led to the second floor. The room at the top of the stairs had a huge open space like a dormitory, with plenty of room for beds and dressers. At the very end of that space, there was a private separate bedroom. It seemed perfect so he bought it.

Terence got to work immediately, creating the kind of farm he had in mind. Although the work was demanding and included lots of heavy lifting and left little time for anything else, he didn't care because he now owned his own place. He was constantly busy with the farm. Despite his very focused attention, however, he was distracted by a petite, young brunette while buying some necessities in town. He didn't recognize her as a local, but she did gain his interest. They ran into each other on several other occasions until a friend finally introduced them. Her name was Honora Fitzpatrick. They seemed to enjoy each other's company from that first meeting and so began a very warm relationship. Within a year, they were engaged and planning a wonderful future on Terence's new farm with the roomy house.

After their wedding, their number quickly increased to three with Ann's birth in 1911. They continued having children until the birth of John Joe, which made a grand total of fourteen children. The large independent family was supported by the cows and chickens they raised, as well as their potatoes and other crops. Like most homes of that era, the house was warmed by the peat in the fireplace where they cooked, that also provided soft lighting. They had no running water but a very reliable well, not far from the house. In a few years, their daughter Sheila, the McGovern's dark-haired, brown-eyed child, was in charge of fetching that water. Her birth was sixth after Ann, Patrick, Alice, Terence, and Pete but before Hugh, Kathleen, Helen, Cody, Brigit, Tommy, Michael, and John Joe.

Life on the McGovern farm was busy. There was so much to do and so many to feed. They were innocent young people in a very rural setting. The children were a mixture of their dark-haired mother and their blond father. When the announcement of a new baby was made, all the children ran around the house searching for the stork. They had a strong faith in God and always believed that He would provide, but just in case, they worked very hard too.

As the older children came of age, they left Cavan in search of opportunity. They left for a better life, but also to aid their parents in raising so many children. Since their father had made the trip years ago, Ann and Alice, the eldest female children, decided to head for New York

City too. On the other hand, several of the boys set out for England, which was just a ferry ride away.

Eventually, Sheila, John's future wife, realized she too should make her move and find her way. Frightened but acting brave, she left the farm at the tender age of seventeen and set her sights on England, where she would join her older brother Pete, who lived in Manchester. He had let her know that jobs were plentiful there. Looking forward to having family close by, she decided to join him. The plans were in place but leaving was even harder than she had imagined. She loved her Mam and Da, but her father owned a special place in her heart. Each time Mam gave birth, she would stay in the parlor for a few extra days, so Da would take over the cooking. He made delicious soda bread, and he was so attentive to the children as they tried to assist him with all the chores around the house. These memories stayed with her forever.

All she knew and loved was centered in this small home in Cavan. Her parents, brothers, and sisters provided all the love and support in her life so she wondered how she could leave them. Despite a heavy heart like so many before her, Sheila woke up on the appointed day, dressed, and bid her warm and loving family goodbye. She took a ferry and moved to Manchester as planned, not knowing if she would ever return, one of the sorrows of many Irish emigrants. Leaving home came with no promises. Many prayers, hopes, and dreams left with them, but no assurances.

Though lonesome and lost, there was a saving grace in her new place of residence: Pete lived nearby and assisted her in every way that he could. Of course, it was still strange, but his welcoming attitude and generosity made the transition bearable. Sheila found a position in a large home, caring for children and working around the house, but she was never quite comfortable. Pete was wonderful, but she found herself thinking about her older sisters in New York. She wondered if they had made a better choice.

Frequent letters traveled from England to Ireland and then to New York, keeping all abreast of the changes in their lives. Within a year, a surprise note arrived from Mam saying, "We expect a new baby in March. Why don't you come home and be the godmother?" Sheila jumped at the chance to see her family again and immediately let her parents know that she would be honored. Once March rolled around and the new baby's birth was announced, she let Pete know about the birth. Teresa, who would be known as Tessie, was an exciting addition to the clan. Her brothers were shocked but delighted to hear there would now be fifteen McGovern children. Sheila prepared for her trip right away because she didn't want to miss a moment of the excitement as so many returned home. She gathered her papers and checked the schedule for ferry departures. Finally, she let her parents know when she was returning, packed, and let her boss know about her plan.

Sheila was thrilled to return to Ireland and her family. When she finally reached the farm, she was surprised that little had changed because her own life was totally different now. Perhaps, she was also different after living a full year in England. Spending time with her brothers and sisters was wonderful. Their voices and warm welcomes renewed her confidence. These faces were the ones that she had watched during her first seventeen years, and they were people she could always trust. Of course, she was also honored to be chosen as godmother to Tessie, child number fifteen. The comfort of being where she belonged was unmistakable. She enjoyed seeing friends and neighbors, but eventually, she had to return to England.

Once she was back in Manchester, she again considered the prospect of joining her sisters in New York. She was so interested that she wrote to immigration and requested to come to the USA, but she was turned down for a variety of reasons. It was the 1930s, during the Depression, so getting a job was next to impossible. Thousands were out of work, so the requirements for sponsors were very demanding. She had listed her married sister, Alice, and her Aunt Nellie as sponsors. The government seemed to look more favorably on married sponsors. Since Sheila's aunt had had no previous contact with her, the authorities doubted she would support her niece if necessary. They also expected sponsors to have substantial savings so that the burden wouldn't fall on America. These strict demands were a way of limiting the number of immigrants who could come in. Disappointed but not totally deterred, she waited again.

Within a year, Sheila gave it another try. This time, she received a much different response. Alice and Aunt Nellie were now acceptable as sponsors and she was asked to send additional information. She completed the paperwork, submitted the necessary documents, and planned for the next chapter in her life. England had been interesting and had shown her another way of life, but it wasn't her final destination. Frightened yet excited, she wrote to her parents, explained her next move, and hoped they'd approve. Though nineteen years old and living independently, Sheila was still their child in her mind. She bid Pete a grateful goodbye. Without him, life would have been very lonely. Finally, she notified her employer and set sail for New York.

John's passport picture from 1930

The new house Jeremiah built

Some of the Lyne children in school in 1910

Honora and Terence McGovern

The first trip to Ireland

Terence McGovern

Chapter 7

The Young Irish in New York

Sheila McGovern arrived in New York approximately seven years later than John Lyne. Though still a very busy city, it had a different atmosphere. The depression changed the look of some parts of the city. Some people were forced to live on the streets because they had lost their jobs and homes. Others stood in breadlines, hoping to find some food. Though it was still a big city with many people rushing from one place to another, there was a sense of desperation. Then, just as people felt they were moving beyond the depression, a recession began in 1937. The tough times continued, and Sheila arrived at this moment. Although it was not as bad as a few years earlier, jobs were hard to find, and many had lost hope. Because she was an optimist, Sheila felt this couldn't last forever in a country with such a wonderful reputation. She had faith that with time, things would improve, including her own life.

After the Great Hunger in Ireland in 1847–52, many Irish people had flocked to New York to survive. At one time, it was believed that there were more Irish people in New York City than in Dublin. Thus, many of their children grew up there. Signs of their existence were everywhere. Archbishops of the Catholic Church bore Irish names, as did many previous mayors of the city and definitely many policemen. At times, all this was a comfort, but Sheila needed more reassurance.

Luckily, she had family to greet her. Her sisters Alice (now a wife) and Ann were living in the city. They were delighted to add yet another sister to their ranks. In addition to family, Ann was interested in introducing Sheila to many of the young Irish people in the city. One of Ann's favorite places was an Irish dance hall that she frequented on Saturday evenings. In fact, Ann had met a very charming young man named Chris Lyne, John's younger brother, and the two seemed very fond of each other. That was also how Sheila met John.

The first Saturday after Sheila's arrival, the two sisters had planned to head for the dance hall together. They went, but the line to enter the hall wrapped around the block, obviously a very popular place. When they were finally admitted, Sheila was amazed at the size of the dance hall. She had attended dances in England while she was there, but none were as crowded or as large as this one. Chris, the baby of the Lyne clan, who had lived with his older sister Mary for a number of years, immediately joined Ann and Sheila and brought over his big brother, John, to meet the newly arrived Sheila. Though a bit shy at first, Sheila eventually relaxed and enjoyed the company of these young gentlemen. They all shared a few laughs. Others stopped by this Kerry-Cavan group, who seemed to be having such a good time. Some were from home (Ireland) and brought their friends along to meet the new arrival.

After chatting a while, Chris and Ann slipped onto the dance floor, and within minutes, a large group stopped dancing to admire them. Sheila was among their many admirers. Ann always had a great sense of rhythm, but this young man was also very light on his feet. Awhile later, John asked Sheila to dance. He, too, was very comfortable on the dance floor. Later, Ann whispered to her sister, "These Lyne men are admired all over for their dancing." After observing both men dancing, Sheila wasn't surprised that their reputation was well known. Both couples continued to have a good time as the night of dancing went on and as many old and new faces came by. Sheila enjoyed the few that she recognized from Cavan, but she was also very careful to note John's friendly behavior toward everyone he met.

Despite his challenging youth in Ireland, John was very comfortable with most people and had a very positive attitude. His early years didn't damage him but only made him much stronger. He missed his family and regularly sent part of his pay to Kerry, but New York offered so much that he was determined to enjoy every part of it. He sought out the education that he had missed at home and gained a diploma here. He had a good job, lived independently, and looked forward to the future. Of course, it didn't hurt that he was also very good-looking. The evening seemed to be going very well. Eventually, Sheila excused herself to use the restroom, but she didn't return for quite a while. John asked Ann to check and see if Sheila was all right, but Ann couldn't find her. The very independent young Sheila had left the dance and made her way home alone.

John walked over to Chris and reported that Sheila seemed to have disappeared. He was upset and a bit hurt that she had left alone. He wondered, "Did she get home safely? Was she upset by something I said?" Later, Sheila admitted to Ann that she didn't want John to feel obliged to take her home just because Ann was with Chris. Her worries were pointless because John felt no obligation to take care of her, but he was interested in getting to know her. When they all met the following week, John let Sheila know his feelings, and somehow, things went very smoothly from that point on.

Things were going so well for Chris and Ann that to everyone's surprise, they were engaged within a few months. It was the second wedding for the McGovern clan because Alice was married already, so Cavan, London, and Manchester were all kept informed on every detail. Many members from the Kerry clan were also living in New York and were pleased to help with the plans. John and Sheila were asked to be the best man and maid of honor for Ann and Chris, so all four were caught up in the wedding plans.

The event itself was a great success, and they all had a grand time. Pictures of these couples in their beautiful gowns and impressive tuxedos were treasured for a lifetime. From that time on, John and Sheila spent a great deal of time together. Sheila had impressed this young man with her interesting conversations and quiet demeanor. She noticed John's outgoing style and admired his easygoing manner. The match was made, and they, too, were married in 1941. Again, the Lyne and McGovern families would join hands and trust that New York would bring the happiness they sought. They had all left a small island in Europe and had traveled three thousand miles to meet in this big city.

Before their wedding, John and Sheila took a train ride all the way up to the Bronx to find an apartment. John felt that the rents were very high, but after discussing some of the positive elements about the apartment, he changed his mind. They chose a one-bedroom, third-floor apartment at 3138 Bailey Avenue, which had been built just seventeen years earlier. Mary Murphy, John's sister, and her family lived in the same neighborhood. They also had several friends in the building, which convinced them they'd be comfortable in this neighborhood. The depression was officially over, and life was very promising.

John and Sheila's wedding

Chapter 8

The Kenmare Connection

After their wedding, the couple moved into the apartment on Bailey Avenue in the Bronx. John had a steady job, and Sheila loved decorating their new home. As time passed, they presumed a third member would join their ranks, but it didn't happen. They kept busy with daily chores, work, and anything that life introduced to them, but that longing never ceased for Sheila. She made numerous visits to the doctor, asked questions constantly, and prayed. Finally, the news changed almost five long years later; they were having a baby, and her life became almost magical.

She would begin one task but quickly drift off, dreaming of the future and how her life was about to improve. When chatting with family or friends, she could barely control the temptation to blurt out the news, but she and John had made a pact to keep it to themselves until they hit the three-month mark. This self-control demanded an incredible amount of strength, but she kept her word.

Over the last few years, she had fretted over her inability to conceive. She discussed it with her sisters and friends and sought advice from her doctor, who instructed her to take up smoking to relax, which was a common belief in 1945. Although she followed his advice and somehow managed to avoid inhaling, there were no results. The tension was enormous, and it all appeared futile. Because they were the products of large Irish Catholic families, they presumed that children would be part of their lives. When it didn't happen, she ultimately felt defeated.

Now, life had shifted. After trying so long, they were finally going to have a child. Her dreams were becoming reality, and she could barely contain her excitement. As she told her husband, John, "Life has already provided such blessings, and this baby is truly a gift from God." John rejoiced along with her and looked forward to the baby's arrival.

So Sheila went about the usual chores of cleaning the house, preparing meals, and paying bills. Even dealing with the dull, everyday business of life brought a smile to her face. When it was time to shop for groceries in a place where she might inadvertently run into neighbors, she had to steel herself to avoid revealing their secret. In fact, she did meet several people that she knew, but she managed to keep the conversation short under the pretext of being in a hurry. She wondered how long she could keep it up.

In the spring when she finally shared her announcement, it was a pleasure to rejoice with everyone. Her sisters Ann and Alice, who were both mothers themselves, were overjoyed. Having been her confidants all these years, they understood the dark moments that she had endured and the helplessness that she felt in her inability to bear children, so they were delighted to share in her happiness. She told her sister Alice, "It seems like a miracle. We had almost given up after so long. Wait 'til Mam hears." Although she was unwilling to share her last few years of struggling with her mother, she was pleased to write to her about this joyful news.

Even neighbors heard about the planned arrival. Many afternoons, Sheila Lyne and Sheila Madigan, a pregnant neighbor, had long conversations as they moved toward motherhood. They discussed physical changes, information they had gained from others, and the best buys in maternity clothes. Sharing tidbits about their pregnancies and expressing anxieties about the upcoming event gave comfort to both women.

Everything was going well for Sheila and John. The apartment was transformed in preparation for the baby. A crib and small dresser were tucked in the corner of their bedroom, and tiny outfits showed up in occasional unmentioned shopping bags.

On a beautiful day in early May, Sheila returned from grocery shopping, unpacked a number of brown bags, and started dinner: a ham, which was one of John's favorites, a few spuds, and some fresh string beans to complete the meal. She was busily paring the potatoes when she heard John's key in the door. As he entered the kitchen, his face revealed the angst in his soul. He remained quiet and avoided eye contact, but she refused to be ignored. In response to her questions, he merely grunted. Desperate but without a place to turn, he finally blurted out, "I was fired today, Sheila."

She stepped back, instinctively covered her mouth, and stared for a moment while trying to comprehend what he had said. With a tear rolling down her face, she asked, "Why? Dear God, I doubt any man on that dock is stronger or works harder than you. Why would they let you go?" Shocked, she couldn't control the barrage of questions that were spilling from her lips. Beneath her verbal queries, her thoughts raced around the financial reality and the child expected in September. They had some savings but not enough to last very long. This pregnancy would prevent her from getting a job, and she had planned to buy beautiful things for the new baby.

Eventually, John continued. "Jim Leahy was fired today, and we don't know why. It's so unfair, Sheila, to lose your job with no explanation. No one expected it, and once the word got out, we spoke of nothing else all morning." He walked over to the kitchen chair and sat down. He was so disappointed with himself and life. When he resumed, he seemed to be reliving the experience. "The more we talked, the more heated the discussions became. It's such an injustice. He has a wife and kids, and now they are left empty-handed. Some of the men thought it was only fair to speak up for him, so Tim, Pete, and I led a protest."

"You led a protest?" Sheila repeated. "You left your job?"

Defensively, John responded, "I don't know if I was right, but it appeared wrong to ignore the poor man's predicament. As we picketed the dock, we tried to gain a larger voice by speaking to the other men, but before we could gather enough men, the boss called us into his office and fired us." The lighthearted warmth that had always filled their small apartment evaporated. They had come to New York for success, happiness, and financial opportunity. At that moment, it was slipping through their fingers.

The news was too shameful to share. Shaken by the enormity of their situation, yet determined to manage it in a reasonable manner, they reviewed their circumstances over and over. For days, every conversation concerned their finances and the way that they should proceed. "How long will our savings last?" Sheila asked John. "Do you think one of your brothers could get you a job?"

Of course, John had the same questions, but he was determined to resolve the situation himself, without his family's assistance. This proud Kerryman couldn't share his humiliation with siblings, but he was too embarrassed to mention this to Sheila. Instead, he merely replied, "The first order of business is to cut way back on spending. No extras." They had never been extravagant, except where the new baby was concerned. Now that, too, would change.

Very quietly, John pursued every possibility for the next few weeks. He spent his evenings with the help-wanted ads and took the subway into Manhattan every morning, seeking any type of position. The jobs that seemed most attainable in the paper had many men applying and all vying for the same opening. Though the war had not ended, soldiers returning home were given priority to honor their service. Others knew someone who was employed by the company, which gave them a leg up, but John had no connections.

These wearying, unproductive days led to evenings of distressed conversations with Sheila. They wondered what they would do. Because asking family members for a loan was out of the question for several reasons, they were forced to find another solution—they would have to borrow from the bank. It was a rather American response to the problem, and it made these independent Irish immigrants uncomfortable, but they had no choice.

After numerous discussions planning how they might approach the loan officer, they summoned all their strength and walked to a local bank on Broadway. Although they were at home in this Bronx neighborhood, they were fearful about revealing their secret, so they proceeded on the north side of the street—the less traveled sidewalk— to avoid contact with someone who might innocently question their destination. Once inside the bank, they approached the administrative offices, and they were introduced to the manager, Mr. Hague. They had brought along all their financial papers, so they explained their situation to him. John kept reassuring Mr. Hague that he would be employed as quickly as possible. He had been a farmer in Ireland, so he was accustomed to hard work. At that moment, the problem was finding a job.

Although polite, Mr. Hague appeared rather distant, which made it difficult to assess his reaction. He left his desk several times, which unnerved the young couple. Nevertheless, they tried to remain positive. On his final return, he sat and asked, "Do you understand your obligations if I grant this loan?"

John replied, "Yes, I understand." He went on to warn them of the consequences if they failed to repay it. The formality of his words and the tone of his voice were alarming. In the end and after all the warnings, he granted the loan. John squeezed Sheila's hand and whispered, "We're safe for the moment." They signed the necessary papers, shook hands with Mr. Hague, and departed.

Mentally exhausted from this strange experience, they talked for hours before retiring. Determined to find success this time, John renewed his efforts the next morning. He checked the morning, afternoon, and evening papers, left word with the Kerrymen's Association, a benevolent and social organization formed by Irishmen from Kerry, and informed his friends about his loss. Finally, and despite the embarrassment, they shared the news with their families, and they were consoled by their generous offers, but they knew that the only solution was a full-time job. John attended all the meetings of the Kerrymen's Association in hopes of making a contact, but several of the men were in the same position, so he saw little hope of getting a job from them. Each morning he left the house and took the subway to the next possibility that was listed in the paper, and every evening, he returned without a job.

As time went on and no jobs appeared, the couple became more frantic. John had completed many applications but had heard nothing positive. An occasional note mentioned that there might be an opening in the future or thanked him for applying, but none promised a job. It had been two months since their visit to the bank, and funds were getting tight again. August had arrived, and the baby was due in September. They wondered what the alternatives were.

When Monday rolled around, John was again armed with lists of positions. He had the help-wanted sections from various papers stuffed in his pockets. He threw them out as he was turned down. He moved onto the next possibility with as much hope as possible. Once he arrived at the next job posted, a very long line of applicants often beat him to the door. Despite the odds, he joined the group and casually looked around for a familiar face. They were there—the same sad men who had shared many previous lines with him and who had obviously been rejected. His positive outlook was fading, but he had to get a job.

After all his efforts, things still seemed quite dismal, so he decided to attend another meeting of the Kerrymen's Association on the following night. He could see several friends and just enjoy a conversation without stress. That evening as he sat chatting with a few men from Kenmare, the town near his home in Kerry, one of the men waved a friend over and introduced him to the group. His name was Jack O'Sullivan, and because he was another Kerryman, they all had a great deal in common. While some discussed the latest news from their hometowns, John and Jack enjoyed their own chat, discussing what part of the city each lived in at that time. John mentioned that he was living way up in the Bronx but was looking for a job anywhere. Jack replied, "We're looking for a few guys down at *The New York Times*, if you're interested." Shocked, John quickly answered yes and almost burst with excitement. Jack went on to say, "You can shape up [hire for a day] tomorrow night. I'll give you the address and meet you at the entrance to the paper."

"That would be great, Jack. I'll be there whenever you want." Jack gave him the address, and John memorized it right away. When he returned home, he didn't tell Sheila about the job possibility, just in case things didn't go as planned. He merely mentioned he would be out the next evening with a man from Kerry looking for a job.

The next evening, he headed for 43rd Street and hoped for the best. He saw Jack at the entrance, and after greeting each other, Jack asked John to follow him into the *Times's* building. The two men entered through a side door and proceeded down into the bowels of *The New York Times*. Jack certainly knew his way around the place and greeted several men along the way as he moved among the massive machines. John followed him closely, trying to adjust to the noise in that vast cavern. Finally, Jack approached a man with a serious demeanor who appeared to be in charge. They spoke for several minutes, and eventually, Jack introduced John. Tom Sheehan was the foreman for the paper handlers. He looked at John and asked, "You're here to shape up?"

John couldn't answer fast enough, "Yes, sir." He shook Sheehan's hand and thanked him profusely. Tom showed him where to get the necessary gear, and John went to work right away while Jack waved goodbye and headed for his own job. At the end of the shift, Tom inquired if John planned to return. "Definitely," he said emphatically. The night had been demanding, but he learned quite a bit. He could barely contain himself as he headed for the subway.

His life had been consumed by worry, searching, and hopelessness for months, but now, all that was behind him. As he sat in the subway and allowed the idea to permeate his being, he found it difficult to absorb this newfound joy. He rejoiced over the Irish connection and his good luck in coming across Jack O'Sullivan. He considered the fact that his Irish heritage may have landed him a job and vowed to do the same for any Irishmen who needed work. It was a promise that he kept for many years. Although there were many Irishmen working in New York, he had been lucky enough to meet a man from his hometown, Kenmare, who had some power. That made all the difference in the world. Above all, he looked forward to sharing the news with Sheila, who was waiting at home on this warm summer evening.

As soon as he reached the apartment door, he made a conscious effort to be as quiet as possible. With the growing tension of the last few months, Sheila needed all the rest that she could get. He unlocked the door and walked softly into the apartment to avoid waking her. Although she barely heard his footsteps, she struggled out of bed and hurried into the kitchen to greet him and inquire about his search this evening. He had just opened the refrigerator when she stepped into the kitchen. Before he turned to greet her, he poured her a glass of milk, took out a beer for himself, and announced, "*Slainte*! I shaped up for *The New York Times* this evening, and they want me back tomorrow night. I think we're going to be all right."

Chapter 9

A Growing Family

John shaped up at *The New York Times* for several months and finally landed a full-time job as a paper handler. It included a forty-eight-hour workweek, with eight hours of overtime built in. He was beyond delighted. They had no more financial worries. When they repaid their loan, the pressure just slipped away. In addition to that good news, Helena Honora Lyne came into the world. She was the answer to their prayers. She was a hearty, healthy nine-pound-twelve-ounce baby. It seemed that life couldn't be any sweeter.

Of course, the christening included the whole family: John's brothers and sisters, any spouses that had recently joined the family, and all their children, as well as Sheila's sisters, their husbands, and their children. Ann, Sheila's oldest sister, was chosen as the godmother and Richard, John's brother with whom he had arrived in New York, was asked to be the godfather. Richard had just returned from the Yukon, where he had spent many years searching for that pot of gold. He returned to New York in 1945 with $20,000, a great deal of money at that time. He spent it in less than a year and left, never to be seen again. Checks that he earned over the years were sent to one of John's sisters, but his disappearance was a loss for all of them.

Other than Richard, family members continued to thrive, and christenings, communions, confirmations, and graduations were frequent, and provided opportunities to admire children, share some news, and have a chat. The men looked forward to the food and a drink or two, as they discussed their work experiences or stories about life in New York. News from Ireland was on the top of the list. Gradually, most of John's siblings reached the shores of America, with the exception of Jeremiah, who stayed on the farm, built a new house with an unobstructed view of the Kenmare Bay, and married Margaret Hampston.

In preparation for the christening, fussing over the menu went on for days. In John and Sheila's home, men were seated first at the mahogany table, which was moved from its usual spot against the wall and fully extended with three leaves in the center of the living room. This arrangement allowed sixteen people to sit rather comfortably at one time. The men were delighted to be the first group served, and they enjoyed the carefully prepared meal that was provided by the hostess. They dove in and enjoyed every last morsel while the ladies walked around the table singing out offers. "More ham, John or Chris?" Sheila might ask.

Alice, while carrying the peas and carrots, might encourage the men with, "These are delicious vegetables, Jim and Richie. Can I give you a few spoonfuls?" More gravy, mash potatoes, and additional vegetables were placed on the table or passed along until the men had their fill. At this point, each man rose, gave great reviews, thanked the hostess, and moved to other seats in the room. By this time, John and Sheila's brothers and sisters had some older children who were seated next. Some were hungry while others were indifferent. Nevertheless, once they were gathered and finally seated, their moms were at full attention and tried to encourage their progeny to behave and eat. Only after everyone else was fed, did the ladies set up the table for themselves. A few minutes to relax and just enjoy one another's company seemed like such a blessing. Every household in the family practiced the same ritual.

In later years, neighbors and long-lost friends from Ireland were welcomed to these gatherings. Some brought instruments for a sing-along while others just relaxed in the warmth of an Irish party. The joy of their abundance from years of struggling was not lost on any of them. The humility of these men ("the in-laws and outlaws," as Sheila would say) was a product of their gratitude. America had provided so much. Hard work, with which they were certainly very familiar, now allowed for these bountiful meals. As the dishes were brought to the kitchen, the singing began. Everyone had a song that belonged to them—like it or not. They all would be called upon to share their special tune. After several had shared their song, John would begin with;

Meet the boys from Kerry,

Meet the boys from Clare,

From Dublin, Wicklow, Donegal

And the boys from old Kildare.

The boys from the land across the sea,

From Boston and New York,

But the boys who beat the Black and Tans

Were the boys from the County Cork.

(McNulty Family, 1937)

Because his mother was from Cork, and he had had his own disagreement with the Black and Tans, this was one of his favorites.

And then the real party would start. Sheila's song was rather heartbreaking. Many viewed her as a sensitive woman, so it seemed appropriate for her to sing such a serious song. It was called "Two Little Children" and told the story of two orphans who died in front of a church while waiting for their mother. It was a very sad song, and although she might complain about singing it, it was hers for a lifetime. Lena, John's sister, always sang "The Connenmara Shore," a beautiful, haunting tune. Despite their love of laughter, the Irish could break your heart with their sad melodies.

The children at the party were also asked to sing. They shyly joined in or fled to another room. Some generous uncles motivated the children with a dollar or two. Sometimes it worked, but others were much too shy to deal with singing for the crowd, even if they were family. There was a dead silence during each performance followed by enthusiastic applause. Their respect for music and poetry was undeniable. It brought back memories of their own parents singing about life in Ireland, so they treasured the songs in their hearts.

These were wonderful years. Yes, an occasional problem might occur, but by and large, the extended family became very American in their aspirations and strove for success in every endeavor. *More* children arrived to fill their lives. Even John and Sheila had another daughter, Diane Marie, and life kept moving forward.

At some point, John decided that the family could use additional income, so he placed an advertisement in *The Riverdale Press* for a gardener (the word *landscaper* had not become part of the jargon yet). He charmed his customers shamelessly on the phone, and when he finished, he calmly told his household, "If I can grow a spud, I can grow a posy," and thus began his gardening career. It was his day job while he worked for *The Times* at night.

The neighborhood included many Irish-born people and Irish-Americans, which was very comfortable for this family. In addition, there were many people from several other countries with unusual accents. After a while, they all became familiar with one another and part of a rather interesting neighborhood. The children attended Saint John's Elementary School, a big Irish parish that held Saint Patrick's Day plays every year. Farther north, Gaelic Park held hurling and Irish football games. Periodically, Sheila and John might attend a game and stay for the dinner dance afterward, but they always brought their children.

Another major holiday in their lives was Saint Patrick's Day. In New York it was everything you've ever heard and more. The Lyne clan's Saint Patrick's Day took on a life of its own. The day began with mass in the morning because it was a holy day of obligation in the New York archdiocese. Before March 17, Sheila's mother would send shamrocks from Ireland, which John placed in the ribbon of his hat on the morning of the parade. He and Helena, their oldest daughter, dressed up early and prepared to join the parade with other family members. They always marched together. This usually meant that they needed a warm coat because Saint Patrick's Day was never known for its good weather in New York City. While they were gone, Sheila cleaned up after breakfast and dressed for the parade. There was no green but only their Sunday best. As soon as they were ready, she and her younger daughter, Diane, headed for the parade. Of course, these trips to Manhattan included a subway ride of about forty-five minutes, but no one cared because it all seemed so thrilling.

Once Sheila and her daughter arrived, they walked over to Fifth Avenue and Eighty-Sixth Street, where the parade turned. They admired the various marching groups and the music as they walked through the crowd of spectators. Marchers could be seen everywhere, either heading for their groups or resting after a long march. The crowds were overwhelming, and the music could be heard blocks away. New

York was truly celebrating its own. Sheila and Diane watched the parade and waited for County Kerry to come up the avenue. At the appointed spot, John and Helena left the parade and joined Sheila and Diane while several family members continued to the end.

The next destination was Lena's apartment, John's sister. She lived in Yorkville on 79th Street, on the east side of the city and welcomed the entire family, as well as friends, every Saint Patrick's Day. When they arrived, the apartment was only half-full because so many family members tried to complete the parade. Sheila and the girls helped Lena with the food as they awaited the additional arrivals. Within an hour or two, the apartment was overflowing with relatives, singers, and an occasional accordion player. The food was plentiful and placed on the table in the center of the kitchen. After the long march, most were ready for a good meal. Occasional political discussions arose with a variety of opinions, but the differences were quickly forgotten once the party was in full swing. When dinner, discussions, and clearing the dishes were over, singing began. The kids ran around like wild people until called upon to share a melody. The night was a delight for everyone because Lena, a single woman, was a little more relaxed, and she seemed to enjoy her nieces and nephews. They loved her too, and they were so flattered when she spoke to them as if they were adults, telling them all about city life. Saint Patrick's Day was always memorable for everyone and another chance to be together.

A big part of John's life was his loyalty to the union and membership in the Kerryman's Association, the place where he had met Jack O'Sullivan. These two organizations occupied his time and thoughts. He often spoke of the benefits of union membership, and how it had changed the lives of the average workman. He never missed a union meeting. On the other hand, the Kerrymen's Association was a more social group which held a number of meetings each year and provided some social interaction with men from home. Always glad to see familiar faces, John also enjoyed welcoming the recent arrivals and making them feel as comfortable as possible. Chris, his youngest brother, was president of the organization for several years.

Sheila's time was spent on family life, especially her children's lives. Homework and the children's success in school were major priorities. Getting good grades and being accepted into a respected high school loomed large in this household. The girls were required to complete their homework immediately after school and right after they had changed out of their uniforms. Although they visited family as often as possible, their daily lives occupied her time. Sheila often recalled her own education in Ireland and the poetry she was required to recite in class. A little tongue-in-cheek at her formal presentation, she struck a very serious pose as she began sharing "Casablanca," a poem about a boy named Casablanca, who refused to leave the burning ship until his father, the captain left.

The boy stood on the burning deck

Whence all but him had fled.

The flame that lit the battle's wreck

Shone round him over the dead. (Hemans 1826)

Sometimes she would share Robert Browning's famous, "Grow old along with me!" Sheila was proud of all the poetry that she knew by heart and was delighted when her daughters were required to memorize poetry—a dying art—but still encouraged in Saint John's Elementary School. Both girls attended Catholic high schools and colleges.

Preparing meals was another important priority for her. Despite the many ethnicities surrounding her, Sheila prepared meals that she was accustomed to, with beef, ham, chicken, and fish leading the way. Grocery shopping allowed some socializing for all the women of the neighborhood, but the arrival of the phone really changed their lives. Sheila could now communicate with her sisters, who lived in Queens, much more frequently. This was truly a blessing. The phone and television changed everyone's life.

Through it all, John and Sheila remained in constant contact with those in England and Ireland. Eventually, John's last few siblings made their way to New York. When Philip, one of the twins came, John was able to get him a job as a pressman for the *New York Times*. He helped many other nephews and friends as well. Later, John's sister Sheila arrived, and she lived with their sister Mary for a while before marrying the always-delightful Austin Mulkeen from Mayo. After spending some years in England, Michael, the other twin, came as well and secured a position with the telephone company.

Sheila kept in contact with her parents and frequently sent money to improve their lives, as most of her brothers and sisters did. But in 1957, she decided it was time to return to Ireland. Almost twenty years had passed since her return for Tessie's christening, and now, she felt a need to see them again. The trip by ship would take one week each way, so they decided to go for the summer. This would be impossible for John because his job would never give him that time off. Nevertheless, John encouraged his wife to go anyway. He felt Sheila's parents were still alive, so it was well worth her while. John's generosity was no surprise. His own parents had passed so long ago but he understood this was her wonderful opportunity. So the planning and excitement began!

For the next few months, Sheila prepared for her long-awaited trip. It would be much more glamorous than her trip to the USA but a little lonely without John. She knew her sisters and his sisters would invite him for dinner often, but he would still feel the loneliness. In preparation for the trip, she began with the Cavan people, her Mam and Da, and wrote to inform them that she was on her way. Next, she wrote to several sisters and John's brother Jeremiah in Kerry. One passport could be used for her and the children, who were eleven and nine years old. She began getting clothes together, but of course, those two kids kept growing and growing. Neighbors warned her that Diane would get very sick in Ireland because she had such terrible hay fever. Sheila took it all in stride. Eventually, June rolled around, and they were on their way.

The ship offered a brand-new experience for all of them, and they enjoyed every minute of it. Lots of family members arrived at the dock to wish them bon voyage, and the girls promised their father that they would keep a diary to record their experiences. Although other members of the family had made the same trip, it was still rare enough to be celebrated. Having so many visitors was great fun, but it gradually dawned on the girls that they wouldn't see their father for months. It was a very late and sad awareness. He, of course, made light of it, but John would miss his family enormously.

Their experience aboard the *Scythia* was much more exciting than they had imagined. From the game room to the costume party, they were always entertained. So many young people aboard the ship were traveling with their families that every day felt like a party. Fortunately, they were assigned to a table in the dining room with another family, whose husband/father had also stayed home, so Sheila gained an adult companion for the trip over. Every day, afternoon tea was served, and Diane became part of the crew that was serving Coke to all those requesting a soda. Of course, she was never paid, but she got a big kick out of working with the crew members. As predicted, the trip took a week and they finally landed in Cobh. Leaving the ship with two trunks and seven suitcases was an extraordinary feat for Sheila, but with the assistance of a porter, she managed it very well.

Once they disembarked, they still had quite a distance to travel. Next, they headed for the train to Dublin. After they boarded and found their seats, all three immediately went searching for the dining car, where tables covered in white tablecloths and set with lovely china awaited them. When the waiter arrived, Sheila requested tea all around. He poured the tea from a silver pot, impressing all of them, but he especially delighted the girls. After they had eaten, they returned to their seats, and the children fell asleep, but Sheila did not. She was so excited and nervous that she could barely sit. In a few hours, they arrived in Dublin, but they still weren't home. Sheila planned to stay at the Gresham (on her bucket list), so they spent the night where the Irish swells often stayed.

The next morning they got in a taxi with all their luggage and headed for their final destination; Bawnboy, Cavan. Sheila had tried to keep her parents informed of her itinerary, but some portions of their trip took more time than she expected. Now she wondered if they'd be expecting her. Would Tessie and John Joe, the two youngest siblings, still be there? Would she recognize the farm as soon as she saw the front gate? As they drew closer, Sheila began to cry, and true to form, her children did too. Then suddenly, they were next to the front gate of a farm, and four people were waiting and also crying; Mam, Da, Tessie, and John Joe. They had taken turns watching the road all morning. The three New Yorkers exited the taxi, joined Mam and Da, and asked a load of questions in between tears. It was a wonderful welcome back for Sheila and a mixed bag for her children, who didn't want their Mom to be upset.

They spent nearly two months at the McGoverns, often visiting her brother Cody's family, who lived close by. Fortunately, most of Sheila's siblings from England and Wales decided to visit. Sheila was delighted to see all their lovely faces. Pete, the brother who had been so kind when Sheila was in Manchester, arrived with his wife, Freda. Michael was welcomed along with his wife, Gladys. She was born in Wales where they currently resided.

As the summer weeks passed, they anxiously watched for the next arrival. There were so many people to meet since some brought children as well as spouses. When each of Mam's children arrived, they spent time in the parlor with her before joining the rest of the family. These were important moments for her and that child, catching up on each other's lives and strengthening that bond that letters just couldn't achieve. The spouses must have been overwhelmed by the attention, but no complaints were uttered. Hugh and his wife, Kitty, came to visit. Bridgie brought her husband Michael, toddler twins, and baby Eileen in a carriage. Kathleen came in a stunning royal-blue suit. She was greeted by Tessie, who quietly made everyone feel at home. Terence, an older brother, joined John Joe and the two men became the comedians for the summer.

Over the span of two months, the house was full of McGoverns and their families. The sleeping quarters on the second floor managed to hold most of the guests. Sheila's children spent days assisting (or following) Da on the farm with Terence and John Joe. In the afternoons, Helena and Diane brought the men their tea in the field which gave them a few minutes to relax before resuming whatever task the farm demanded. The cows had to be milked, which the girls soon learned was not an easy task. Hay had to be dried and placed in haystacks. Helena and Diane joined in all these activities, and in the evenings, they learned to play cards with John Joe and Terence. The girls also tried to keep their promise to their father and maintain a diary, but it was difficult to keep up. While trying to retrieve a memory, they could frequently be heard wondering, "What happened yesterday?"

The adults were so tired of the question that they would just respond, "It rained." Despite their forgetfulness, they wrote to their dad every week and tried to make daily entries in their diaries.

Life on the farm was delightful. All the male visitors, whether they were blood relatives or had married into the family, helped Da on the farm. The daily chores kept everyone busy, particularly when there was so much company. The occasional conversation during a busy day became special for those few moments. Talking to their sister, after such a long time, was a pleasure for all involved. Some had been very young when Sheila left. Tessie had been an infant, and Sheila was only eighteen when she returned home for the christening, so they never had an adult conversation. Now Sheila was thirty-seven, and Tessie was a young woman. The good feelings from that summer brought them all closer and endured for the rest of their lives. In years to come, many of Sheila's siblings and their children made the trip to New York, and they were warmly welcomed.

Although the chats were fabulous and spending time with her brothers and sisters might never happen again, the visit had to end. Sheila had promised to spend two weeks with John's brother Jeremiah, who now owned the family farm in Kerry. That farm was in the south of Ireland, and it would take some time to get there. So Sheila began packing their clothes and gathering various belongings for Kerry. She said goodbye to each of her siblings and their families as they left their parents' home, and now, she had to say goodbye to her parents. Mam and Da were in great shape and still active on the farm, but she wondered how long it would last. Staying so long had relaxed her into a routine, and she was slightly shocked to have to say goodbye again. Sheila spoke to each parent with tears in her eyes, packed up the kids, and got into a taxi from town. They returned to Dublin and took the train to Killarney. Again, they hired a car and made their way to Jeremiah's farm.

The southwest of Ireland had a totally different look when compared to the flatlands of Cavan. Kerry was mountainous, and had beautiful scenery, but Cavan's level land was much more conducive to farming. Jeremiah and his family were very welcoming. Even better, they had children about the same age as Helena and Diane. Family members were warm and welcoming, even though they had never met Sheila before. Their easygoing style made the visitors so comfortable that the two weeks flew by.

Raising sheep was native to these mountains, and Jeremiah was adept at caring for them. In a calm tone, he would instruct his sheepdog to bring the sheep down from the hill, and the dog immediately ran up the mountain and behind the sheep, barking furiously. The creatures fled down the mountain to escape the dog and gathered on the field in front of the house. Once they arrived, Jeremiah would usher them into another field, with the assistance of the dog. But the most exciting event took place when the sheep had to be sheared. Each creature was handled individually. None of them seemed to enjoy the process. The wool was a very profitable part of the farm. The visitors from New York were fascinated. In addition to the sheep, Jeremiah raised cows, pigs, and chickens, which kept the entire household—his wife and five of his six children—busy.

But Jeremiah's true strength was his charm. He escorted the family on private tours through parts of the ring of Kerry, led sing-alongs after dinner, took the family to Kenmare, and revealed many hidden secrets about the town. He was a delightful man and leaving him and his family was as emotional as their previous goodbyes.

Finally, returning to New York was wonderful. This voyage provided the trip of a lifetime, but now they were anxious for home. Losing one parent for months made these girls appreciate their father. Everyone on board the ship was excited to see New York Harbor. As soon as the girls saw their father, they began to cry as they realized how long it had been since they were together. It was so wonderful to be home. Sheila and John had written to each other all summer, expressing their loneliness, and looking forward to this moment. The reunion was an awakening for all of them.

Chapter 10

Life in the Bronx

Resuming their lives took a little adapting for each member of the family. John was delighted to see delicious home-cooked meals return, which Sheila promptly resumed. When they all sat for dinner, with John at the head of the table, it was a treat for him to be surrounded by a loving family. He might make the occasional gesture, indicating he was about to get up because the salt or some other necessary item was missing, but someone else always grabbed it first to avoid disturbing John's dinner.

The girls were a week late for their school's opening in September, but fortunately, their teachers were very tolerant. Nevertheless, they were a little nervous because they had never missed a day of school without a full medical diagnosis. Elementary school was very demanding in the 1950s, and Saint John's Elementary School had high standards. Notebooks had to be purchased, books must be covered, and new book bags and pencil cases bought. Of course, that was nothing compared to the work that they had missed and had to make up.

When Sheila returned, she was anxious to get in touch with her sisters and let them know how the family in Ireland was doing, especially their mother and father. The parents they left behind many years ago had grown older, and the youngest children were now adults. It had been a pleasure to listen to John Joe and Terence, who were two very funny, delightful men. Ann and Alice wanted to hear it all, and they enjoyed every word that she shared.

Once they had been home for a few months, John and Sheila began to consider a move to a bigger apartment. Sheila introduced the topic just after Helena's twelfth birthday at the end of September. One Saturday, Sheila mentioned, "I think it's time for us to look for a new place."

Surprised by her remark, John responded, "Why would we leave this apartment?"

Sheila explained, "I think we need more space now that Helena is twelve years old, and Diane will turn ten on her next birthday."

John thought about it for a moment and observed, "The girls seem pretty comfortable to me. Do you really think that's necessary?"

"Well, I think they need their own rooms, with a little privacy. We don't have to go far away; in fact, I'd prefer a place nearby so we won't have to pull them out of Saint John's," she added. After giving it some thought, John agreed.

They shared their plan with a few neighbors and asked friends to keep an eye out for an available apartment. They even mentioned it to the superintendent in their building. After several months of searching, they were told about an apartment at 3055 Bailey Avenue. When they saw it, they were very pleased to see three bedrooms. The master bedroom was much larger than the one they had now and so was the kitchen. The girls could share a bedroom, and John who still worked at night, could sleep in the interior third bedroom during the workweek, since it faced the back of the building where there was less light and little noise. They quickly agreed to the terms and looked forward to their new home. Another bonus of this move was that Philip, John's brother, was able to take over the old apartment. After the new place had a fresh coat of paint, the family moved in.

The girls were also delighted with the move because their friends were just up the block. In many ways, life stayed the same. Jobs, school, and friends all continued, but now there were new neighbors and friends. The girls were growing up. As the 1960s rolled in, high school and a whole new stage of life were on the horizon. Helena had been an excellent student throughout elementary school. At graduation, she received a history medal, so her parents had very high hopes for her future. She attended the Academy of Mount Saint Ursula, which was highly recommended, but the family chose it for a different reason. The Ursulines, a religious order of excellent teachers, were very proud of their standards, but Sheila was unfamiliar with them at the time. She had her own reason for their initial visit.

On a typical Saturday morning in late fall when Helena was in the eighth grade, Sheila awoke to a freezing apartment. The first thing she did was contact the superintendent, who informed her that the system was being repaired but it might take all day. Despite the bad news, she prepared John's breakfast and lunch while wearing a warm sweater. This was John's sixteen-hour day and she made sure there was plenty of food to last the entire day. When he left for work, Sheila wondered how she and the girls would get through a Saturday in an apartment with no heat. Once the girls awoke, she asked Helena to find the flyer she had brought home from school on the previous day. Helena dug through her book bag and retrieved the paper that described the Academy of Mount Saint Ursula—its reputation and the many programs it offered. Sheila immediately announced, "We're going to this open house at Mount Saint Ursula to stay warm." The girls were agreeable, so they took the bus and spent the day there.

Much to Sheila's surprise, Mount Saint Ursula was a wonderful school, and the presentation by the principal convinced her that this was the place for her daughter. As with all Catholic high schools at that time, you could apply anywhere, but you had to be accepted to attend. The COOP (Cooperative Admissions Exam) helped Catholic schools make that decision. Helena was accepted, and the family was delighted. High school had a major influence on Helena's life, so there was never any doubt that the family had made the right choice.

In addition, another very practical matter arose. Once Sheila and the children had returned from their trip, some of their relatives decided to come to the States, a very exciting notion for the entire family. One particularly noteworthy arrival was Helena and Mary Ann Lyne, Jeremiah's oldest daughters. They didn't come for just a visit; they planned to stay in New York. Several relations, including Sheila, John, and Diane, were at the airport for their arrival. The girls were teenagers and nervous as they took this big step to leave their family in search of new opportunities. Sheila was especially sympathetic to their situation, although the girls were not her blood relatives. Recalling her own arrival in New York, she understood their apprehension as they faced the unknown. She was particularly kind and warm to these young women as they made their way in New York. She loved having them visit whenever possible.

Everyone in the Lyne family invited them at some point, but life here was very different from their experience in Kerry. The crowded streets, new and unusual faces, and no nuclear family were frightening facts for these very young women. Their situation was similar to those who had arrived a generation before. The girls made the best of it and gradually relaxed into their newfound home. Helena (now there were three Helena Lynes) was quieter, but she became talkative once she was comfortable. Mary Ann, on the other hand, had a great sense of humor and enjoyed her new relatives, flaws and all.

But as the family faced this new era, something more vital to their survival was changing. Within a few years, the newspapers and the transit authority were going through growing pains. Automation seemed to threaten several unions, and many feared that their jobs might disappear. The pressmen took the lead and went on strike, which closed the newspapers for almost four months, during 1962 and 1963.

The *New York Times,* where John was employed, along with several other newspapers closed during this strike.

For the Lyne family, this meant no income. Of course, they didn't know how long the strike would last, so they had to prepare for the worst. Helena, a senior in high school at the time, had a job at Woolworths and kept teasing her parents that she was keeping them alive. The truth was that John and Sheila had always conserved their resources and had enough savings to pull them through. It was a long battle, but they were able to cope due to their careful management, a lesson they had learned much earlier. Mike Quill, another Kerryman and the president of the transit workers' union, waged the same battle with the transit authority. John knew several men who were employed by the transit authority. They understood that this wonderful American dream could end, so they were truly grateful when all these threats were over. John returned to work just as Helena graduated from high school.

The Lyne family continued to thrive on Bailey Avenue as the years slipped by. They dealt with the good and bad and managed to survive and even thrive. Life had been good and Sheila and John were glad to share their happiness with their family and friends.

Sheila and John at Diane's college graduation

Chapter 11

John's Trip to Ireland

Life was moving quickly. New York City was changing, and their family was making major decisions. Both girls attended Catholic colleges. Helena majored in nursing, but after two years, she decided that it wasn't the profession for her—a decision she later regretted. Diane was pursuing a degree to become an English teacher, a profession that Helena joined years later in Norway. With his children practically grown, John did a little soul-searching and realized that if he ever planned to return to his native land, it was time. He was fifty-seven years old, and he could retire in less than eight years.

Ten years after Sheila's last trip, they decided that it was time to return to Ireland before they were too old. So in 1967, they planned a trip to England and Ireland. Sheila's father had died earlier, and at that time, she flew to Ireland several times to say goodbye. She had spent a lifetime loving and admiring her father, so she needed to see him face-to-face to say goodbye. Now her mother was living in the suburbs of London with her youngest brother, John Joe, and most of her siblings lived there too. They planned to stay in London, near Sheila's mother, for several weeks and then travel to Ireland. The itinerary was set, and all the relatives were notified. John was returning to Ireland! When he boarded the plane, someone casually inquired if John was just returning from his first trip to New York City. She must have overheard his strong Kerry accent. Without a moment's hesitation, John replied, "Yes, I've been visiting for thirty-seven years." The inquirer was astonished.

The first stop was London. John, Sheila, and their daughter Diane set off for Sheila's sister Bridgie's house on Saint Anthony's Road in London. She had very generously invited the New Yorkers to stay with her while in London. It was a wonderful first stop because her four daughters were grown but still home. Tessie, Sheila's godchild, was living with them as well. This was also John's first meeting with the rest of Sheila's family. Sure, he knew her sisters in New York, Alice and Ann, but there were many more people to meet, beginning with his mother-in-law, who was now staying nearby. Bridgie was a wonderful hostess and invited other members of the family often. Some evenings, Bridgie prepared dinner for a gang, and a gang showed up, and were welcomed. Michael, his wife, Gladys, Terence, Pete, Freda, John Joe, and many others came. Other nights, they all set out on a walk to explore the area. On one of those evenings, John reprimanded Sheila for walking too fast because her mother couldn't keep up. John was obviously trying to win over his mother-in-law, twenty-seven years into their marriage. The Yanks also stayed with other members of the family. Pete, his wife, and his children welcomed them into their home too.

After three weeks, they were off again for Kerry. This was the ultimate return for the man who had wonderful memories of his home, despite the difficulties he had faced in childhood. While living in New

York City, he spoke of Ireland as though it were paradise. Now he would make his return visit. They stayed in Kenmare and took a car out to Jeremiah's place. When they arrived, they were greeted by a very warm Margaret Hampston Lyne, Jeremiah's wife, who offered them a cup of tea immediately. Sheila and Diane had met Margaret on their last trip to Kerry, but John was meeting her for the first time. As the women had discovered in the past, she was as welcoming as before. Jeremiah had some business to tend to, so Margaret and her guests strolled out to the fields, and John remembered the Irish names of each field, although it had been thirty-seven years. Everyone was astonished at his memory, but farming had been his job for years during his youth, and he had spent a great deal of time cultivating each field. Those memories and the sight of all the animals on Jeremiah's farm warmed his heart. It truly felt like home.

Just minutes later, a man suddenly came over and started chatting. John wondered who this could be and asked his name. The man looked him in the eye and responded, "It's me, Jeremiah." Absolutely astonished and embarrassed John had to walk away. He was astounded that he hadn't recognized his own brother. Thirty-seven years later, they both looked very different. It was an emotional moment, but within minutes, they were all laughing. This was the toll of such a demanding life— these men were unable to recognize those who were so important in their youth. They visited their parents' grave and prayed for their peace, a common practice in Ireland. Except for Daniel, who had died, and

Jeremiah, who owned the farm, the Lyne family members had all settled in and around New York and had created new lives. Being reunited with his brother was more significant than either man realized.

They all spent time watching and assisting Jeremiah around the farm. John and Jeremiah recalled the Puck Fair and the time when they lost Mam's money. Now it was fun to think back on those years and dismiss the struggles of the past. They truly enjoyed each other's company. Jeremiah pointed out the changes he had made on the farm, including a two story, brand-new house. They even spent some time strolling through the remnants of the old stone home where they had grown up. It was still standing on Jeremiah's farmland. So much had happened since John left.

Several nights later, they had a party in Smith's Pub, and people came from great distances to greet John. He had become a farmer at such a young age that many twenty to thirty years older felt a kinship with this former child farmer. The place was quite crowded, and John was delighted. He saw faces that he hadn't seen in many years. Thanks to his brother Jeremiah, it was a wonderful night. There was singing, stories, and recitations while an accordion occasionally played in the background. Conversations took him back to a time when he was responsible for the farm and thus knew many of the farmers by name. These men had labored on the land and produced what they could for survival. But times had changed, and they were all older and grateful for the lives that they had chosen. In talking to John, they recalled how he and his brothers were determined to make the farm a success. The night was wonderful as many old friendships were renewed. John was so sorry to see the evening end, but these memories would last forever.

During the day, John visited the fields and walked the entire farm. He loved the beauty of the land and the mountains just behind the fields. Kerry was exceptional. He wondered if he could or should have stayed there. He did miss Ireland and his parents, but certainly, what he had found in America had enriched his life beyond his dreams. With Sheila, he had established his own family, and his daughters had made him very proud. In addition to them, he had a good job to support them and one that had allowed him to make this trip back home. Most of his siblings lived nearby in New York, and he saw them often. Jeremiah had stayed in Ireland and built a new house to welcome his bride. He, too, had found a great deal of happiness in his family and in being a farmer. All of them had chosen a successful path. He thanked God that it had been an easier life for most of them.

The two weeks flew by, and once again, John had to leave Ireland, but it was under much different circumstances. He had his wife with him, who spent a good deal of her time fussing over his clothes to make sure he was "presentable," as she might say. He appreciated her interest and enjoyed the attention. Diane, who was now a junior in college, was with him, and they were returning to Helena who now worked full time. Seeing Ireland again and recalling his experiences brought the past into sharper focus. Losing a father as a boy and his mother as a young man had been his most challenging moments. Although he enjoyed many parts of his youth in Ireland, maintaining a farm had been a tough road. Luckily, his brothers and sisters were always right beside him, supporting him, working for a better life, and sharing an occasional laugh. They were the stuff Ireland was made of. Being surrounded by people who loved him then and now made this trip a success.

Epilogue
Helena

Because John and Sheila waited five long years for their first child's arrival, her miraculous birth brought untold happiness. They adored her. From a very early age, her preferences were made clear, particularly her taste in food. She was fussy. Because she rejected most food and was so skinny, Sheila feared people would think she wasn't being fed. The child knew what she liked immediately and shared that information with her parents on numerous subjects. Bearing the name of both grandmothers, Helena Honora had inherited an Irish will of steel that would last a lifetime.

Their high expectations proved fruitful as they observed her moving from grade to grade. Always an excellent student, her success in school made them continuously proud of her accomplishments. For instance, she loved the orderliness of mathematics and found it pleasing to master problems. She made it her business to absorb her homework, regardless of the time it required, and she plugged away at chemistry and Latin until she understood them thoroughly. Helena was every parent's dream. Her achievements proved to John and Sheila that America was truly the land of opportunity.

By the time she was fifteen, Helena had grown to a whopping five feet, ten inches tall. Her father's people were known for their tall, strong women. John's mother, his Aunt Phyllis, and her daughters were quite tall. Helena had met these young women on her first trip to Ireland. That early experience exposed her to the benefits of height in a woman, so she was pleased to grow as tall as possible. Eventually, many of the friends that she made were the same height or even taller. As a group, they were very comfortable together, which only increased their confidence. They were all attractive young women, and their height was a point of interest, but it never interfered with their social lives.

Although demanding of herself and of life in her early years, she became quite introspective in her later teenage years and sought to improve herself in every way. She chose to be the best person that she could be. Unlike most teenagers, who are absorbed with just their appearance, she tried to improve her soul as well. Oh, she still loved clothes and took every opportunity to find just the right outfit, but she also made new choices in her behavior. She paid close attention to her teachers, absorbed their philosophies, and tried to follow their advice. It may have begun with Mother Winifred, the speech teacher at Mount Saint Ursula who implied that a Bronx accent wasn't desirable (Who knew?) and instructed students to imitate the Nebraska A in Johnny Carson's accent. It made sense to Helena to try to improve every facet of her life. She began working on her speech but realized that those improvements could go far beyond speech and into all aspects of life. It all appealed to her. She was always a good person, but now, she chose to be kind, and the change was impressive.

On a more practical level, like her parents, Helena loved to travel beyond the borders of home, seeking a more interesting lifestyle. Although they were driven by need, Helena's goal was to see what else the world had to offer. Her curiosity was as powerful as their need, and she felt compelled to follow it. The wanderlust that appeared to be part of her DNA may have sprung from the stories that had been shared over the years by aunts and uncles who had left Ireland and England, seeking better lives.

Once Helena decided to leave nursing school at Seton Hall University, she moved into her own apartment in New York City for a short time and shared many of her experiences in Manhattan with her family. She encouraged them to see some of the wonderful theater available in the city. *Da* was one of her favorites, and her parents loved it. Her next move was Washington, DC, where she completed her bachelor's degree in anthropology and spent time with her cousin Noreen. This developed into a very close and long-lasting friendship in their adopted home. In a couple of years, however, Helena moved to Seattle, which was a bit gloomy for some, but all that rain reminded her of Ireland. She travelled to several other states to see what they offered and found some exciting and new ideas. By the time Helena returned to New York, she had fallen in love with skiing, and whenever time allowed, she could be found on the slopes of Hunter Mountain and many other skiing locations.

About this time, Sheila noticed a tremor in John's hand and suspected that it might be Parkinson's disease. Members of his family had been diagnosed with this illness in previous generations, so it wasn't really a shock to him. John and Sheila visited a neurologist for a final diagnosis, and it was determined that he did indeed have this devastating illness. John kept his position at the *New York Times* for the next five years, but the disease kept progressing. Although he fought against it for years, he gradually realized that he would have to retire.

During those early years of John's diagnosis, Sheila was so busy caring for her husband that she barely noticed that she had lost weight due to a difficulty with swallowing. When she finally went to a doctor, she was told that she had cancer of the esophagus. Her husband's needs had consumed so much of her attention that she had ignored her own situation. That neglect would have catastrophic results. Within a short time, surgery was performed at Columbia Presbyterian Hospital and was considered a success. For the next two years, life continued in a somewhat normal manner as Sheila still focused on John's needs. However, the third year changed all that because the tumor returned. Helena, who was working in Orange County, took a leave of absence from her teaching position to take care of her parents. She moved back to the Bronx and helped them get to doctors' appointments, eased their anxiety, and generally made their lives more comfortable. Without her, life would have been impossible.

By that time, their grandchildren had entered the world, which brought them a great deal of happiness. Since their other daughter lived in Rockland County, they decided to leave the city that they had called home for so many years and find an apartment in Rockland County near Diane, but Sheila never moved in. A week before the scheduled move, Sheila's condition became dire, and she was rushed to Columbia Presbyterian Hospital. Within a short time, Sheila died in the hospital at the age of fifty-six. During her illness, she frequently repeated, "I've had a wonderful life, healthy children, and a good husband." These words provided great comfort to her family as they watched her pass into the next world. Her positive attitude gave some peace to those she left behind.

Helena moved into the new Rockland apartment with her father and helped him deal with the loss. The two sisters shared his care for years, bringing him to rehabilitation centers and senior citizens' meetings with two children in tow. Helena also pursued her interest in skiing. In fact, she met a Norwegian, Leif Iverson, on one of her ski trips. He had skied to school while growing up in Norway but had lived in the USA for some time. After several months, this relationship grew in importance, but unfortunately, Leif was considering a return to his native land because jobs were hard to find in New York. He was a carpenter in Rockland County, and the building trade had almost disappeared.

He asked Helena to marry him, but life was terribly complicated at that time. She considered bringing her father to Norway because he could not be left alone. Despite the obstacles, Helena agreed, and the two prepared to leave for Kristiansand. Helena found someone willing and able to teach her Norwegian, and she made it her business to master it. Always a good student, she was delighted to learn a new language that she would be using in a short time. A few months before their departure, John had a stroke and passed away. He was seventy-two years old. The man who fought so hard to reach the States and find a successful life reached his goal, but it all ended too soon. His optimistic attitude permeated his family's life and brought a great deal of happiness. The difficulties that he endured as a young man only made his success in America sweeter.

Several months later, Helena and Leif flew to Kristiansand, Norway, Leif's hometown. They met his family and later married. Life for Helena was initially difficult. Communicating in Norwegian was more demanding than she had anticipated, and the job limitations were disappointing. But her determination to succeed kept her going. Diane had been teaching for years, and they often discussed the pros and cons by phone. Finally, Helena considered resuming her teaching career. She sent for her credentials, made a number of inquiries, and hoped for the best. Lo and behold, she landed a job, and it was perfect. She loved the interaction with her students, who were English majors in high school. It was a slightly different system from the one in American schools. Eventually, she also earned a graduate degree in Norwegian history, and teaching that history became part of her responsibility.

Helena spent over twenty-five years in Norway, growing accustomed to the culture, getting to know Leif's family, and enjoying life. This young woman, the child of parents who came to America to find their happiness, searched even farther to fulfill her dreams. Hopefully, they all found the dreams they were seeking.

25 first cousins gathered at Bridgie's 80th birthday

References

Blackwell, Ann Hackney, and Ryan Hackney. *The Everything Irish Irish History and Heritage Book*. Avon, Massachusetts: Adams Media, 2004.

Fitzgerald, Mairead Ashe. *A Terrible Beauty: The Poetry of 1916*. Book review: *The Irish Times,* August 19, 2015.

Hemans, Felicia Dorothea. "The Boy Stood on the Burning Deck." *The Monthly Magazine*, edited by John Aiken. London, vol. 2, August, 1826.

Lyne, Gerard. *The Lansdowne Estate in Kerry Under W. S. Trench, 1849–72*. Dublin: Geography Publications, 2006.

Lyne, Gerard. "Tuosist Landholders in 1698." *Tuosist 6000*. Kerry, Ireland: Tuosist History and Newsletter Committee, 1999, pp. 128–140.

McKeown, Marie. "Blood of the Irish: What DNA Tells Us about the Ancestry of People in Ireland." Owlcation, 19/08/2018. https://owlcation.com/stem/Irish-Blood-Genetic-. . . Identity.

McNulty Family. "The Boys from the County Cork." London: Decca Records, 1937.

Pearse, Padraig. "The Rebel." *Padraig Pearse: The Collected Works.* Dublin: Maunsel and Roberts Ltd., 1922.

Smithson, Michael A. "The Mayburys of County Kerry." https://www.bing.com/search?q=Maybury%20county%20Kerry&FORM=ARPSEC&PC =ARPL&PTAG=5320 #:~:text=English%20Civil%20War.-,https%3A//sites.rootsweb.com/~mabry/kerry2.html,-Images%20of%20Maybury.

Yeats, William. "A Drinking Song," *The Collected Poems of W. B.* Yeats, revised 2nd edition, edited by Richard Finneran. London: Scribner Paperback Poetry, 1989, pp. 93–94.

Yeats, William and Lady Gregory (Isabella Augusta). "Cathleen Ni Houlihan." *The Collected Plays of W. B. Yeats.* Dublin: Samhain, February 18, 1907.

Made in United States
North Haven, CT
23 November 2022

27151062R00109